The Illustrated
BOOK OF
HERBS

Gilda Daisley

The Illustrated
BOOK OF
HERBS

Gilda Daisley

With illustrations by Ingrid Jacob

AMERICAN NATURE SOCIETY PRESS
New York

This 1983 edition is published by
American Nature Society Press, a
division of Arlington House, Inc.,
distributed by Crown Publishers,
Inc.

Printed in Spain by
Graficas Reunidas.

Library of Congress Cataloging in Publication Data
Daisley, Gilda.
    The illustrated book of herbs.
    1. Herbs.   2. Herb gardening.   3. Cookery (Herbs)
I. Title.
SB351.H5D34   1983   635'.7   82-18220
ISBN 0-517-40027-8

CONTENTS

INTRODUCTION

There can be few tasks more rewarding and therapeutic than growing and preparing your own herbs. It is a sad fact that there are still many more herbs imported to Britain than are grown here even though, with a little care, most herbs, although more suited to the Mediterranean, will survive happily in a northern climate. Herbs are fascinating plants to grow and each has its own traditions and folklore as well as its individual medicinal and culinary uses.

One of the earliest herbals was written over 5000 years ago in China and contains over a thousand cures. The Egyptians and Babylonians used herbal remedies at about the same time and from then onwards their popularity grew; at one time there was no distinction made between culinary and medicinal herbs.

In the sixteenth century Paracelsus, a German propounded the Doctrine of Signatures, now known throughout the world. It works on the principle that like cures like – eg, plants with heart-shaped leaves are good for the heart, plants with red flowers are good for the blood etc. Some plants are even named after the condition that they cure – eg, eyebright, liverwort and heartsease. The most famous British herbalist was Nicholas Culpeper (1616–1654) whose "Compleat Herbal" is still in print today.

All that is essential for growing a few favourite herbs is a 2 m (6 ft) square of garden – failing this, a sunny window ledge will do. Choose a sheltered sunny position, if possible by a south-facing wall, and prepare the soil well by digging thoroughly and forking in plenty of humus. Heavier clay soils will need to be lightened and dug over several times before any planting is done. Ideal soils for growing herbs will be those that retain a certain amount of water yet at the same time are well-drained as herbs do not like to have wet roots. Most herbs love lime so, if necessary, add some to the soil a few weeks before planting and replenish each year. Once the herbs are established, fertilize them sparingly for too rich a soil will provide lush, rapidly-growing plants but this will be detrimental to their flavour and perfume.

It is preferable to use fresh herbs in most recipes, but dried herbs can retain some of their essential flavour if care is taken. Herbs for drying should always be picked in the morning when they are freshly open and after the dew has evaporated from them. Always choose those with perfect leaves and flowers and place them on a screen made by stretching some light material such as net over a frame and securing it at the edges. The screen can then be stored in a dry, airy place such as a shed or garage where there is plenty of air circulating on all sides of it.

Alternatively spread them on a warm, dry shelf but remember to turn them frequently to ensure even drying. A third and very successful method is to tie the herbs in bunches and hang them, head downwards, in a kitchen or garage until dry but take care that they are not in a position where they can be attacked by damp and condensation. Bunches can be protected by a "sleeve" of cheesecloth (muslin). Check the drying herbs frequently and once you are satisfied that they are quite brittle, snap off the leaves and flowers from the stalks and store them in screw-topped glass bottles for use throughout the year. Although very useful in the winter months, dried herbs do have a limited shelf life and after about a year will lose their flavour and perfume.

Some herbs are more suited to freezing than drying e.g. chives and parsley which when dried, rapidly lose their unique flavour and deteriorate. Chop them finely and freeze in tiny plastic bags, enough for one dish's requirement at a time. Do not refreeze or mix the different varieties of herb in each bag.

In most cases, freezing is a better way of preserving a herb's unique flavour. There are three methods.
1. Chop each herb finely (with chives, dill and basil use kitchen scissors which are less damaging). Pack separately into ice cube trays, top up with cold water, then freeze. Turn out the cubes into polythene bags (spraying them with soda water should prevent them sticking together), then label and return to the freezer. You can take out cubes as required.
2. Best method for large quantities of popular herbs such as parsley, mint and tarragon which are used in sauces and stuffings. Liquidise each one separately in a blender with a little water. Pour into small containers to freeze. The blocks can be added to a dish without being thawed first.
3. Collect small bunches of each herb, rinse under gently running water and shake dry. Wrap bunches in freezer film or foil, pressing out as much air as possible, label and freeze. When needed, crumble the frozen bunches straight into the food.

Herbs frozen by any of the above methods can be stored in the freezer for 6 to 9 months.

Because dried herbs can become musty with long storage, they shouldn't be used in dishes that are going to be frozen. Use fresh herbs if possible; if not available, add dried herbs when the dish is being reheated. The general rule is to use one third the amount given for fresh (eg, 1 teaspoon/5 ml dried instead of 1 tablespoon/15 ml fresh).

Artemisia dracunculus

TARRAGON

Family: Compositae

'It sweetens the breath, dulls the taste of medicine.'
– John Gerard

This indispensable culinary herb is named after Artemis, the Greek goddess of hunting and of virginity, although ironically some forms of tarragon were once believed to induce abortions. Its second botanical name, *dracunculus*, means 'small dragon', and to the fanciful the plant's long thin leaves could be seen as tiny dragons' tongues. Tarragon originates from the Middle East, and grows wild by rivers and streams in central and southern Europe and in parts of North America. There are two main types: Russian or 'false' tarragon (*A. dracunculoides*) and French or 'true' tarragon (*A. dracunculus*). The former is a tough plant and easy to grow but it lacks the distinctive bitter-sweet flavour of French tarragon which makes the latter variety the perfect addition to many culinary dishes and the one which is particularly worth growing. It is easily distinguished from Russian tarragon by its strong fragrance and its shiny olive-green, rather than bright green, leaves.

The plant is a half-hardy perennial which will reach 60 cm (2 ft) in height by the end of the summer and can spread to 90 cm (3 ft) in width. The tiny, greenish-white flower buds appear in early summer but in Britain, unless the weather is very warm, they will not open properly.

Cultivation

When selecting a new tarragon plant, choose one whose leaves have a delicate aniseed fragrance, and beware of seed-grown plants, which can prove almost tasteless. Plant in the spring or early autumn when there is no danger of frost and always select the sunniest spot available. The type of soil does not matter – tarragon will even thrive on stony land – but the one thing the plant cannot stand is having wet roots, so if your soil is full of clay, try to choose a bank or slope to ensure adequate drainage. In the late autumn cut the plant back to about 5 cm (2 in) above the ground and cover with straw or dried leaves and grass to protect it from frosts.

Tarragon tends to lose its flavour as it gets older so propagation should be carried out every year or every other year in order to have a continuous supply of fresh young plants for the kitchen. One way of doing this is to select the more robust suckers that surround the plant in the spring, separate them from the parent plant with a sharp spade and replant them directly into the ground. Keep them moist, particularly when just planted, and they will develop a strong enough root system during the summer to survive the winter. Alternatively, in the summer take cuttings of the young stems, about 10 cm (4 in) long, including a portion of heel at the stem base, and pot these indoors using a light potting compost to which a handful of lime chips has been added. Do not fertilize more than once a month. It is better to be frugal than lavish with the feeding – an over-enthusiastic dressing of nitrogen-rich fertilizer may well cause the roots to shrivel and die. The plants will, however, need plenty of water, good drainage and a sunny position. By the following spring they should be well-rooted and can be planted out.

Uses

No kitchen should be without tarragon. Harvest the young leaves and shoots before the flower buds develop, when the plant is at its most aromatic and yields the greatest amount of natural oil, dry them as quickly as possible at a constant temperature of about 35°C/95°F and keep them stored in airtight jars.

Tarragon's distinctive taste makes it an essential ingredient in many dishes but its delicate flavour will be swamped if it is used with other strongly flavoured herbs, such as thyme or rosemary. For the same reason it should not be cooked for more than a few minutes or should be added to dishes just before serving. Individual leaves make good decorations for cold savoury dishes, particularly those prepared in aspic such as chicken and sea-food. Tarragon is also delicious when finely chopped and added to mayonnaise or to hot and cold soups.

TARRAGON VINEGAR
Sprigs of fresh tarragon to fill 0.5 litre (1 pt) jar
2 strips lemon rind
1 clove
White wine vinegar

Pack the jar loosely with tarragon, add the lemon rind and clove. Pour on enough vinegar to fill the jar and allow to stand for a month, shaking occasionally. Strain and bottle. A branch of fresh tarragon can be added to the bottle to give a stronger flavour and looks particularly attractive if the bottle is green.

TARTARE SAUCE
This makes a delicious accompaniment to fried or grilled fish and to grilled steak. It is easy to make and the home-made variety has a far more subtle flavour than that of commercial types.

1 shallot
6 sprigs fresh tarragon
3 sprigs fresh chervil
15 ml (1 tbsp) capers or pickled nasturtium seeds
1 gherkin
2 egg yolks
2.5 ml ($\frac{1}{2}$ tsp) dry mustard
Salt and pepper
5 ml (1 tsp) wine vinegar
150 ml ($\frac{1}{4}$ pt) olive oil

Chop shallot, tarragon, chervil, capers and gherkin very finely and put in mixing bowl. Stir in the raw egg yolks and mustard, and season well with salt and pepper. Very gradually add the vinegar, stir well, and add the oil a little at a time. Store in the refrigerator.

TARRAGON AND EGG TARTS (serves 4)
225 g (8 oz) shortcrust pastry
25 g (1 oz) butter
25 g (1 oz) flour
300 ml ($\frac{1}{2}$ pt) milk and cream
15 ml (1 tbsp) chopped fresh tarragon
Salt and pepper
4 eggs

Roll out the pastry thinly and line four 10 cm (4 in) tart tins. Prick well and refrigerate for 30 minutes. Bake blind at 220°C/425°F (gas 7) using baking beans or cooking foil to cover the bottom, until the pastry is set. Meanwhile, heat the butter and stir in the flour to make a smooth paste. Gradually add the combined milk and cream, bring to boil and cook gently for 2 to 3 minutes until smooth and thick. Stir in the chopped tarragon and season with salt and pepper. Keep hot, stirring occasionally. Break an egg into each pastry case, return to over and bake at 180°C/350°F (gas 4) for 15 minutes. Cover with the hot sauce and serve immediately.

Tarragon

Valerian officinalis

VALERIAN

Family: Valerianaceae

'It is under the influence of Mercury and therefore has a
warming facility.'
– Culpeper

This small, insignificant looking plant has been used for thousands of years as a medicinal herb. Its name comes from the Latin *valere* – to be healthy – and it has long been popularly known as 'all heal'. A tisane made from its roots acts as a tranquillizer and according to the English herbalist, Nicholas Culpeper, it will work with the speed of mercury on the body's whole nervous system. With such rare properties, it cannot be blamed for not also being useful in the kitchen or for its unattractive appearance, although cats often find the strong, rancid smell of its roots irresistible – hence the plant's other nickname, 'cats valerian'.

Valerian can be found all over Britain and Europe, growing in damp places such as the banks of streams and ditches or grassy woodlands, where it may reach a height of 60–90 cm (2–3 ft). The light-green, sharply divided leaves are feathery and droopy, and the pale pink flowers, which appear from June to late August, are in rounded clusters, each floret pouched at the base.

Cultivation
Valerian seeds are slow to germinate and you should allow for a 50 per cent success rate. Sow the seeds sparsely in late spring, pressing them gently into the soil but not deeply, so that they have maximum warmth without being completely covered; to assist germination cover them with cloches. Once the seedlings have developed, transplant them to their permanent growing position, which should be sunny but damp and, as with all herbs, well drained. Valerian will also respond to container growing,

provided that the drainage and moisture of the soil is maintained. If valerian is being grown purely for its rhizome, the flowers should be nipped as soon as they appear and the rhizome should be dug up in the autumn of its second year.

Uses
The top of the plant is full of phosphorus and is useful on the compost heap where it will rapidly turn to humus. This can be put on the vegetable garden to protect the soil from erosion, extremes of temperature and fungicidal diseases, as well as to improve the drainage. The rhizome, with its sedative properties, should be stripped of its straggly roots, sliced and left to dry off slowly, which can be done on screens made of stretched muslin or on shelves. Remember not to dry it too close to the house if you want to avoid the unpleasant smell. Once dry, the slices of root will be brittle and can be ground and stored in screw-top jars.

VALERIAN TEA
This soporific tea will not produce unpleasant side-effects like some commercial sedatives do, and is very beneficial in providing a natural sleeping draught at times of special stress. It should not, however, be taken as a regular cure for insomnia and if insomnia persists, always consult your doctor.

Into a cup of warm milk blend 5 ml (1 tsp) of dried valerian root which has been pounded using a pestle and mortar. The strong taste can be offset by adding 5 ml (1 tsp) of honey or brown sugar.

Valerian officinalis

Rosmarinus officinalis

ROSEMARY

Family: Labiatae

'See the much Rosemary, and bathe therein to make thee
lusty, lively, joyful, likeing and youngly.'
– William Langham, 1579

Rosemary is another of the herbs introduced to Britain by the Romans and this sweet-scented plant is still particularly loved today by the Italians and the British, who use it frequently in their cooking. In ancient Greece and Rome rosemary was believed to strengthen the memory, which accounts for it being known as the herb of remembrance and fidelity. A sprig of rosemary was often placed in a bride's bouquet or worn at funerals, and those taking examinations would twine rosemary into their hair or massage rosemary oil into the forehead and temples. This may well have worked, for rosemary stimulates the circulation, increasing the blood supply to the brain. Rosemary is also said to ward off infection and protect men and women from the forces of evil, and apart from the traditions associated with it and its many culinary, medicinal and cosmetic uses, rosemary makes an attractive addition to the herb garden.

The plant is native to the Mediterranean but although it prefers coastal conditions, it has been known to thrive as far inland as the Sahara Desert. A perennial shrub, rosemary has spiky, evergreen leaves which are dark and glossy on the upper side and grey-green and downy underneath. The small, blue nettle-shaped flowers appear in May to June and are a great attraction to bees. The shrub will grow to 120–150 cm (4–5 ft) and a few bushes planted together will make a compact, fragrant hedge.

Cultivation

More at home in the Mediterranean than colder climates, rosemary requires a sheltered spot in which to grow – a south or west-facing wall is ideal – and light, limey but above all well-drained soil. Seeds are difficult to germinate as well as very slow to grow and the best way to propagate rosemary is either by cuttings or from layering. Cuttings of 10–15 cm (4–6 in) should be taken in early summer from a ripe, flower-free shoot; remove the lower leaves and place the cutting in water or dip in hormone rooting powder and plant in a rooting compound such as vermiculite until the roots have formed. Alternatively, a new plant can be easily produced from an old by firmly pegging down a small branch into the soil with a piece of wire or twig until the roots are established and then removing it carefully from the parent plant. Keep the young plant moist but not too wet as the roots easily rot. The new plants should be transplanted in early autumn to allow them to harden off before the winter, and they may need to be protected with straw where winter conditions are severe. Once established, rosemary bushes do not like to be moved. If this is attempted, the leaves will often turn brown and die, so if it is necessary to transplant try to avoid cutting any roots when doing so and retain as much of the original ball of earth as possible. If happy in its position, rosemary can last for about 30 years. Trim it lightly to maintain its thickness.

Rosemary also makes an excellent indoor pot plant and if carefully pruned forms a very attractive bonsai plant. Once a cutting has formed a good ball of root, pot it in a mixture of sand and potting compost, taking care in handling the delicate roots and retaining as much rooting compound as possible. Allow it to become slightly pot-bound at this stage, which will encourage flowering, but do not overdo it. If, however, the plant becomes too pot-bound, remove the top growth to ease the strain on the root system.

Rosmarinus officinalis

Uses

Rosemary has long been known for its therapeutic powers. Try placing a sprig under the pillow of a sleeper who suffers from nightmares – it often produces a miracle cure. Both rosemary oil and rosemary tea have many uses and the herb makes an excellent skin tonic and astringent as well as a hair conditioner, not to mention a delicious flavouring in food.

ROSEMARY OIL

Rubbed gently onto the skin, this will help calm the nerves and increase the circulation, and a few drops added to the bathwater will help bring relief to those suffering from rheumatism.

400 ml ($\frac{2}{3}$ pt) almond oil
15 ml (1 tbsp) white wine vinegar
Sprig of fresh rosemary (bruised)
2–3 juniper berries (optional)

Fill a prettily shaped 0.5 litre (1 pt) bottle with the almond oil, vinegar, sprig of rosemary (washed and carefully dried) and juniper berries. Leave on a sunny window ledge for a month or, if the weather is cold, place the bottle near a warm radiator or in the airing cupboard.

ROSEMARY TEA

This can be used as an aid to digestion and taken at bedtime as a soothing drink to calm the nerves and induce sleep. Use about 15 ml (1 tbsp) of crushed rosemary leaves – fresh are better than dried – per cup of boiling water.

HAIR CONDITIONER

This recipe, much prized by gypsies, has an excellent conditioning effect on the hair, preventing dandruff and even, it is alleged, curing baldness. To make it, take a bunch of fresh rosemary and crush or chop the leaves; add 300 ml ($\frac{1}{2}$ pt) boiling water and allow to stand for an hour, then strain. Use it as a final rinse after washing and towel-drying the hair.

When used in cooking, rosemary should be added to the dish at the beginning so that its full aromatic flavour can permeate the food slowly. It should not

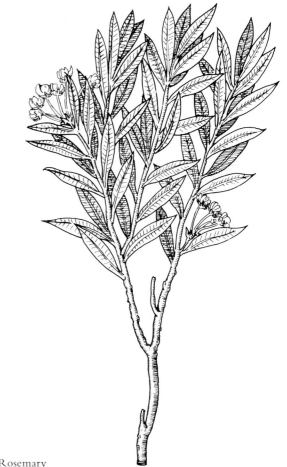

Wild Rosemary

be used uncooked because of the texture of the spiky leaves and woody stem, nor in large amounts because of its strong flavour, reminiscent of incense or pine. Some cooks prefer to place the rosemary in a firmly tied muslin bag before adding it to a dish; others simply tie a bunch of rosemary together and add it as it is. Since little of the flavour is lost when the herb is dried, use either fresh or dried rosemary, whichever is more convenient.

VEAL CASSEROLE WITH ROSEMARY
(serves 4)

700 g ($1\frac{1}{2}$ lb) pie veal
15 ml (1 tbsp) flour
Salt and pepper
30 ml (2 tbsp) olive oil
1 large onion, chopped
125 g (4 oz) button mushrooms
225 g (8 oz) canned tomatoes
2.5 ml ($\frac{1}{2}$ tsp) dried rosemary
150 ml ($\frac{1}{4}$ pt) dry cider
1 small carton sour cream or natural yoghurt

Trim the excess fat from the veal and cut into small pieces. Coat well in flour seasoned with salt and pepper. Heat half the oil in a large frying pan and brown the veal in it. Remove the meat from the pan, add the remainder of the oil and fry the onion in it until transparent. Add the mushrooms and sauté for a few minutes, then add the tomatoes and rosemary and stir in the cider. Bring to simmering point. Return the meat to the pan, cover and cook at 180°C/350°F (gas 4) for 1–1½ hours until tender. Just before serving, stir in the sour cream or yoghurt and heat through without boiling. ·

BAKED PORK WITH ROSEMARY AND LEMON (serves 4)

Olive oil
Fillet of pork, about 700 g (1½ lb)
1 lemon
Freshly ground black pepper
Sea salt
4 sprigs rosemary

Heat the oil in a frying pan and brown the pork rapidly on all sides. Remove from pan and place in a baking dish. Finely grate the lemon rind, taking care not to add any white pith, and sprinkle over the pork. Season with sea salt and black pepper. Squeeze half the lemon juice on to the meat and place the sprigs of rosemary on top. Cover and bake in a pre-heated oven at 190°C/375°F (gas 5) for 40 minutes. Remove the rosemary before serving and reserve the juices to use as sauce to accompany the meat. Serve with rice or potatoes and a green vegetable.

ROSEMARY WHOLEMEAL BREAD

This is delicious served warm with butter and cheese or as an accompaniment to soup.

15 g (½ oz) fresh yeast or 10 ml (2 tsp) dried
2.5 ml (½ tsp) sugar
300 ml (½ pt) tepid water
350 g (12 oz) wholemeal bread flour
5 ml (1 tsp) salt
30 ml (2 tbsp) fresh or 15 ml (1 tbsp) dried
   rosemary

Activate the yeast by mixing it with the sugar and 15 ml (1 tbsp) of the water and leaving it covered in a warm, draughtfree place for 15 to 20 minutes until frothy. Add the remaining water to the yeast. Sift the flour into a pre-warmed bowl, add the salt and most of the firmly chopped rosemary leaves. Make a well in the centre and gradually incorporate the yeast into the flour until a dough is formed. Take the dough out of the mixing bowl and knead it on a lightly floured surface for about 7 minutes. Return to the bowl, cover and leave to rise in a draught-free place for about an hour, until it has doubled in size. Turn out on to a lightly floured surface and knead for a further three minutes. Place in a well-greased 0.5 kg (1 lb) loaf tin, cover and allow to prove in a warm place until the dough has risen to the top of the tin. Lightly brush the top of the loaf with milk and sprinkle a little crushed rosemary on top. Bake in a pre-heated oven at 240°C/475°F (gas 9) for 10 minutes, then reduce the heat to 190°C/375°F (gas 5) and bake for a further 30 minutes or until cooked.

Garden Rosemary

Satureia

SAVORY

Family: Labiatae

'Boiled and eaton with beans it forthwith helpeth the affects of
mother proceeding from wind.'
– John Gerard

Summer savory (*S. hortensis*) was a herb popular with the ancient Greeks and Romans. Its piquant taste made it a good accompaniment to fish and meat dishes and the Romans mixed it with vinegar to make a sauce in the same way as we now make mint sauce. The herb is a native of the Mediterranean and quickly became established in Europe after the Romans introduced it. In the Middle Ages it was widely used as a stuffing or accompaniment to meat and game, and since then it has commonly been called 'bean herb' because a few leaves of summer savory added to green beans have a magical effect similar to that of mint on peas.

In temperate climates summer savory is classed as an annual. It grows quickly, reaching a height of about 30 cm (1 ft), and has thick shrubby branches and a stem that is woody at the base. The short stalked leaves are thin and dotted with glands on either side. In June and July the delicate blue and white flowers appear, closely resembling those of lavender and rosemary, and they will last until the autumn, to be followed by fruit formed in tiny nutlets.

Winter savory (*S. montana*) is similar to summer savory in appearance but is a hardy evergreen perennial. Both are strongly aromatic but winter savory has a sharper taste making it slightly less preferable for culinary use. It is, however, a much more robust plant and because of its compact shape and rapid growing habit, makes a good border plant. At maturity it forms a thick shrub about 30 cm (1 ft) high and a short, dense hedge of winter savory to protect the more delicate herbs in a herb garden is useful for both culinary and ornamental purposes. It was often used in this way in the knot gardens of Tudor England.

Cultivation

Savory is easy to grow and will survive and multiply on the poorest chalky soil, although it prefers one that is rich in humus. Winter savory can be propagated by division, cuttings or seeds but it is best to propagate summer savory only from seed. Both varieties like a sunny position and if planting seeds, the soil should first be prepared by digging in well-rotted compost. Rake over the surface several times, removing large lumps and creating a fine tilth, and water the bed for a few days until thoroughly moist. The seeds hould be sown in late spring in rows about 30 cm (1 ft) apart. Cover them very sparingly with soil so that they have the light necessary for germination and also cover them with fine chicken wire as a protection from birds. For maximum effect position the wire 15 cm (6 in) above the seeds so that it is impossible for birds to peck through the holes. If you have any spare cloches, they can be used instead. Once the seedlings are large enough to handle, thin them out to 15 cm (6 in) apart or plant them directly in their permanent flowering position for the summer and autumn.

One or two summer savory plants will supply enough leaves for most people's needs – the leaves should be harvested before the plant flowers when the volatile oil contained in them is at its peak. The leaves of winter savory, however, do not dry successfully and become very hard. If one wants a supply of fresh leaves within easy reach, the plant can also be grown indoors, though it will need a sunny position. Pot it in a rich soil compost, lightly dressed with lime, and give it plenty of water. Trim the young plant well back so that it will become bushy. For a more showy variety of savory which grows well indoors,

Summer Savory

try *S. calamintha*, very similar to winter savory but with large, broad leaves.

Uses

Apart from its culinary value, savory is also useful as a general tonic. A mild tea made with a few crushed dried leaves and boiling water has a pleasant, warming effect and since savory, like rue, is reputed to sharpen the eyesight, use it also to relieve eyestrain due to overtiredness or bad lighting. It will also help to disguise the flavour of unpalatable medicine, and a few leaves added to a bottle of white wine makes a refreshing tonic. In an emergency crushed leaves of savory can be applied to bee stings to bring rapid relief.

SAVORY STUFFED LAMB (serves 4)
The special flavour of savory – hot like pepper but with the tang of sage and a suggestion of rosemary – is especially good as a stuffing for roast dishes.

1.4 kg (3 lb) leg of lamb
125 g (4 oz) fresh breadcrumbs
15 ml (1 tbsp) fresh or 10 ml (2 tsp) dried savory
1 medium onion, finely chopped
1 clove of garlic, crushed
6 juniper berries, crushed
1 egg yolk
Salt and pepper
1 glass red wine
50 g (2 oz) butter
Sprigs of fresh parsley

Bone the leg of lamb, allowing sufficient room for stuffing. Combine the breadcrumbs, savory, onion, garlic and juniper berries with the egg yolk and season well with salt and pepper. Stuff the meat, secure with skewers and string if necessary, place on a trivet in a roasting tin and pour over wine and melted butter. Bake at 180°C/350°F (gas 4) for 1½ hours, basting every 20 minutes. Garnish with sprigs of parsley and serve with gravy made from the pan juices.

SAVORY STUFFING
Savory as the basis of a stuffing for baked fish, particularly trout, is delicious.

75 g (3 oz) butter
15 ml (1 tbsp) onion, finely chopped
125 g (4 oz) fresh breadcrumbs
10 ml (2 tsp) fresh savory, finely chopped or 5 ml (1 tsp) dried
1 lemon
Salt and pepper
1 egg

Melt the butter in a frying pan and gently fry the onion until transparent. Combine the other ingredients in a bowl with the egg and when thoroughly mixed add the onion. Allow to stand for 15 minutes before using.

COURGETTES WITH SAVORY (serves 6 as a side dish)
Bland tasting vegetables such as marrow or courgettes particularly benefit from being cooked with savory.

15 ml (1 tbsp) olive oil
1 large onion, chopped
2 cloves garlic, crushed
450 g (1 lb) tomatoes, skinned and chopped
Small bunch fresh savory sprigs
900 g (2 lb) small courgettes
15 ml (1 tbsp) flour
Grated cheese
Salt and pepper

Heat the oil in a heavy frying pan and sauté the onion, garlic, chopped tomatoes and savory sprigs for 10 minutes. Remove mixture from the frying pan and take out the savory sprigs. Slice the courgettes and toss lightly in flour. Put them in the frying pan and brown in the remaining olive oil. In an ovenproof dish arrange alternate layers of sauce and courgettes, ending with sauce. Top with grated cheese and bake at 180°C/350°F (gas 4) for 30 minutes.

Tropaeolum majus

NASTURTIUM

Family: Cruciferae

'They disperse themselves far abroad, by means whereof
one plant doth occupie a great circuit of ground.'
– Gerard, 1597

This attractive, brightly flowered plant is an asset to any garden, not just for its looks but for its many other qualities. Sometimes known as the 'flower of love', nasturtiums are said to act as an aphrodisiac and to have powers of rejuvenation. They certainly contain viamin C – nasturtium leaves were once used as a cure for scurvy – and sulphur and phosphorus, which makes them valuable on the compost heap. The essence they secrete into the soil acts as a protection for neighbouring plants from pests such as white fly and woolly aphids, and they are also useful in medical and cosmetic recipes as well as in cooking.

The plant is a native of Peru, where it grows as a perennial. In colder climates it is an annual but it grows and spreads with equal ease. There are several varieties and the trumpet-shaped flowers, set off by the round, clear green leaves, may be bright orange, red or yellow and in a few varieties delicately variegated. These will last until late October if the weather is mild. Because of their rapid growth and thick foliage, nasturtiums provide useful camouflage for unsightly fences or sheds, though they can get out of hand and will as happily appear inside a shed as outside.

Cultivation

Provided the soil is light and the position sunny, nasturtiums will flourish. If you are growing them for their leaves rather than their flowers, dig manure into the soil before planting seeds. Sow these in late spring and for the first few weeks water them lightly. After that they will look after themselves.

Nasturtiums also grow well indoors. If you have little space, choose a bush or dwarf variety, such as Tom Thumb; other varieties are ideal for a well-lit porch or conservatory where they have room to climb or hang. Sow the seeds in the spring and use a light potting compost for more flowers or a rich compost for more leaves. Water sparingly and feed with a little liquid fertilizer about once every two weeks. Add a few more seeds every two or three months if you want to maintain a constant supply of leaves.

Unfortunately blackfly are particularly fond of nasturtiums and if this pest strikes, wash the leaves with a mild soap powder or washing-up liquid. Spray later with nicotine sulphate or with a home-made pesticide – 4.5 litres (1 gallon) water to about 50 cigarette stubs, boiled for 30 minutes and then strained. This solution is highly toxic so as with all pesticides keep it clearly labelled and safely stored.

Uses

Apart from the general usefulness of nasturtium plants to the gardener, the flowers look pretty in indoor flower arrangements and both the leaves and flowers can be eaten as they are or added to salads and sandwiches to provide a vitamin supplement. For those who suffer from catarrh and chest infections, an infusion made from 7 g ($\frac{1}{4}$ oz) of finely shredded fresh leaves steeped for a few minutes in 300 ml ($\frac{1}{2}$ pt) boiling water, then strained, will help bring relief. A fresh infusion should be mixed and sipped daily. Crushed nasturtium seeds added to a little hot water and applied as a poultice, held in place with a muslin or soft cotton compress, will help draw a painful stye.

Nasturtium leaves and flowers have a peppery flavour without the harshness and indigestibility of pepper, which makes them useful in the kitchen as a pepper substitute. They can be added to mild egg and cheese dishes or to salads to give them a spicy lift.

Tropaeolum majus

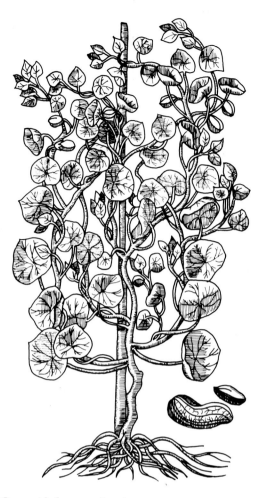

Indian Cress with flower and seed

NASTURTIUM HAIR TONIC
This makes a refreshing hair lotion which can be massaged into the scalp with the fingertips or applied on a hair brush.

75 g (3 oz) each of nasturtium leaves, flowers and
　seeds
75 g (3 oz) young nettles
600 ml (1 pt) alcohol
Few drops of rosemary oil

Mince the nasturtiums and nettles in a household mincer and steep in the alcohol for at least a week. When thoroughly marinaded, strain and add a few drops of rosemary oil (see recipe on p. 14).

NASTURTIUM AND CUCUMBER SALAD
The nasturtium leaves and flowers in this salad not only go well as a flavouring with cucumber but look particularly attractive.

Nasturtium flowers and small leaves
Olive oil
White wine vinegar
1 clove garlic, crushed
Sprig parsley, chopped
Salt and pepper
1 cucumber, thinly sliced

Wash the nasturtium flowers and leaves carefully – they will probably harbour insects – dry thoroughly and shred. Make an oil and vinegar dressing by mixing 3 parts of oil with 1 part of vinegar and flavouring with the garlic, parsley, salt and pepper. Arrange the cucumber slices in a shallow serving dish and cover with the dressing. Surround with nasturtium flowers and leaves, arranged alternately.

VINEGAR WITH NASTURTIUM FLOWERS
This delicately flavoured vinegar can be stored and used long after the nasturtium flowers have disappeared from the garden.

Nasturtium flowers
1 clove garlic, bruised
White wine vinegar

Wash and thoroughly dry enough fresh nasturtium flowers to fill loosely a 600 ml (1 pt) jar. Add the garlic clove and pour in the vinegar until it reaches the brim. Cover the jar and leave to steep for at least a month in a warm dark place. Strain and bottle.

PICKLED NASTURTIUM SEEDS
These make an effective and cheap substitute for capers. The green seeds should be picked carefully because they are easily shattered.

300 ml ($\frac{1}{2}$ pt) white vinegar
15 ml (1 tbsp) salt
3 peppercorns
1 bay leaf
225 g (8 oz) nasturtium seeds

Put the vinegar in a pan with the salt, peppercorns and bay leaf. Bring to the boil and simmer for 30 minutes. Take off the heat and add the nasturtium seeds. Allow to cool, then bottle in sterile jars.

Levisticum officinale

LOVAGE

Family: Umbelliferae

'Being drunk it eases the pains of the guts and swelling of
the stomach.'
– John Gerard

This useful culinary and medicinal herb has a very long history which may go back to the Phoenicians. The ancient Greeks and Romans valued it for its antiseptic properties and it was commonly used in the Middle Ages to cure a wide variety of ailments, from indigestion to boils. The blanched stems of lovage are often eaten in Asian countries today to ward off infection and build up immunity to cholera. The herb has a sharp but pleasant smell which can counter-act less pleasant odours and in medieval times young women about to meet their lovers would often hang a little bag of lovage round their necks in order to smell sweet.

Lovage is a perennial, with dark green, shiny leaves and straight, hollow stems which bear clusters of yellow flowers in July and August. Once established, it will grow up to 2 metres (6½ ft) tall, with deep roots, and because of its height it should be placed towards the back of a border so that it will not overshadow smaller plants. A single plant will be sufficient for one family's needs.

Cultivation

Lovage seeds, like those of parsley, are not easy to germinate and before planting it will help to soak the seeds overnight or keep them between damp blotting paper in the refrigerator for a few days. A shady position is essential for germination and the seeds should be as fresh as possible. Plant them in mid-summer in drills about 2.5 cm (1 in) deep and once the seedlings are beginning to grow, transplant them to their permanent position. This can be done in the autumn or, if the seedlings are not far enough ad-vanced, in the following spring. The plant benefits from a rich, moist soil and the bed should be well dug and fertilized with compost and a few handfuls of bonemeal. Try to wait until the plant is established before picking the leaves or the remaining leaves may die back, and to encourage leaf growth, pick off the flowers. It will take about four years for the plant to reach full maturity.

Uses

Because of its antiseptic properties, lovage can be used to treat wounds and a tea made from lovage leaves has a cleansing effect, particularly beneficial for the kidneys. Lovage also acts as a deodorant and a few crushed leaves added to the bathwater have a refreshing effect. Today lovage is probably of most use in the kitchen. It has a lovely yeasty flavour rather like celery and the blanched stems do in fact make a good celery substitute. Both the leaves and the seeds can be added to casseroles, soups and sauces; the seeds have a stronger flavour so use them sparingly. Young lovage leaves and stalks, chopped and sim-mered in boiling, salted water until tender, make a good vegetable on their own; serve them with butter or white sauce. They can also be used to en-hance the flavour of a green salad.

RED LENTIL SOUP (serves 4)

225 g (8 oz) red lentils
1 litre (1¾ pt) stock
45 ml (3 tbsp) olive oil
1 large onion, finely chopped
1 clove garlic, crushed
60 ml (4 tbsp) chopped fresh lovage leaves or 30 ml
   (2 tbsp) dried
15 ml (1 tbsp) chopped parsley
Salt and black pepper
150 g (5 oz) carton of natural yoghurt

Wash the lentils and remove any grit. Drain well. Bring stock to the boil, add lentils and simmer for 30 minutes. Heat olive oil in a frying pan and sauté the onions and garlic; add lovage and parsley and cook for 5 minutes. Add to the lentils and stock, season with salt and pepper, cover and simmer very gently for a further 15 minutes. Remove from heat and stir in the yoghurt just before serving.

SOUFFLÉ OMELETTE WITH LOVAGE
FILLING (serves 1, or serves 4 as side dish)

2 large eggs
Sea salt and freshly ground black pepper
Knob of butter
10 ml (2 tsp) fresh or 5 ml (1 tsp) dried lovage leaves

Common Lovage

Separate the egg whites and yolks and beat the whites until stiff. In a separate bowl beat the yolks, season with salt and pepper, and add the chopped lovage leaves. Fold this mixture into the beaten whites. Melt the butter in an omelette pan, pour in the mixture and allow to set on the bottom. Loosen the edges and fold over gently. If the omelette is not quite set, it can be placed under a moderately hot grill for a minute.

NORTH AMERICAN LOVAGE SALAD
(serves 4 as side dish)
This makes a delicious accompaniment to cheese and rye bread.

1 large green pepper
6 shallots
15 ml (1 tbsp) chopped parsley
Large handful of fresh lovage leaves
45 ml (3 tbsp) white wine vinegar
90 ml (6 tbsp) olive oil
5 ml (1 tsp) mild mustard
Salt and black pepper
1 crisp lettuce

Remove the seeds and membrane from the green pepper and chop the flesh coarsely. Finely slice the shallots and add to the green pepper, together with the chopped lovage and parsley. Pour over the dressing made from the oil, vinegar, mustard and salt and

pepper. Shake and then chill thoroughly. Wash and dry the lettuce carefully, arrange in a salad bowl and add the chilled mixture.

TRADITIONAL BOLOGNAISE SAUCE
(serves 4)

15 ml (1 tbsp) olive oil
Knob butter
1 large Spanish onion (finely chopped)
2 cloves garlic, crushed
Large handful of chopped fresh lovage leaves
Large handful of chopped parsley
2 sprigs basil
225 g (8 oz) lean minced pie veal
425 g (15 oz) can plum tomatoes
30 ml (2 tbsp) red wine
15 ml (1 tbsp) tomato purée
1 bay leaf
Sea salt and freshly ground black pepper

Heat the oil and butter in a large frying pan, add the onions and garlic and sauté until transparent. Add the lovage, parsley and basil, and cook for a further 5 minutes. Stir in the veal and cook slowly for 10 minutes. Add the tomatoes and their juice and simmer until the mixture begins to reduce. Stir in the red wine, tomato purée and bay leaf, and season to taste. Allow to simmer very slowly for a further 1½ hours. Remove the bay leaf and serve with spaghetti or rice which has been tossed in cheese.

Levisticum officinale

Salvia officinalis

SAGE

Family: Labiatae

'How can a man die who has sage in his garden?'
– Arab proverb

This ancient herb originated in the Mediterranean and is now found in temperate climates across Europe and North America. The Elizabeth herbalist, Gerard, talks of the popularity of sage as a medicinal herb but the plant's therapeutic properties were known long before the sixteenth century. Apart from acting as a general tonic, promoting a long and healthy life, sage is considered a remedy for coughs and colds, constipation, liver complaints and rheumatic pains. Sage tea is still sometimes served in Greek cafes today and in the Middle Ages the Chinese traded their own tea for the sage tea of Europe. The herb has a pungent, slightly bitter but warm flavour and it is generally more valued now for its culinary uses than its healing powers.

Sage is a small, greyish-green evergreen shrub which will grow to about 30 cm (1 ft) in height. It is an attractive plant, with rough wrinkled leaves and spikes of soft purple flowers in the summer, and it requires little attention. There are many varieties, of which *Salvia officinalis* – 'true' or 'garden' sage – is the most common, followed by broad-leaved sage.

Cultivation

Sage appreciates a well-drained, chalky soil and plants, particularly when young, are not likely to survive on water-logged clay soil. If that is your problem, lighten it by digging in some peat and adding a top dressing of lime when preparing to plant. The narrow-leaved variety of sage is best grown from seed and the large black seeds should be planted in spring, when the frosts are over, in drills 2 cm ($\frac{3}{4}$ in) deep. They will be slow to germinate but once the seedlings have reached about 50 cm (20 in) in height, they can be transplanted to their permanent flowering

position. Broad-leaved sage can be grown from cuttings taken in the late summer when the flowers have died. Choose young shoots with a heel of stem on them, and moisten and dip them into hormone rooting powder before potting – vermiculite makes an excellent potting medium at this stage. Let these cuttings establish themselves through the autumn and winter in a greenhouse or by a sheltering wall, and plant them out in the spring. Sage bushes will last for several years but it is wise to have new young plants coming along to take the place of old woody ones.

Sage can be grown indoors as a pot plant but it is essential to place it in a sunny position or it will become leggy, with a cluster of shrivelled leaves at the tips of the woody stems. A good variety for indoor growing is *S. officinalis tricolor*, which is a pretty, upright plant with purple stems and oval, variegated leaves that do not tend to lose their colour as easily as other indoor varieties do. Use a rich potting mix with a handful of lime chips added for drainage and to balance the alkaline. Water sparingly and do not over-fertilize as this will encourage too-rapid growth. Once the plants are established, cuttings can be taken as for outdoor sage.

Sage should be cut back to prevent it becoming spindly and woody. Wait until the second year when the leaves will be rich in natural oils and cut the leaves in midsummer and again in the early autumn.

Uses

Sage and onion stuffing is a combination known even to the least culinary-minded and this strongly aromatic herb – its scent comes from the essential oil, tannins, contained in the leaves – is a useful flavour-

Salvia officinalis

ing in the kitchen. A popular drink in Holland is made by adding a few leaves of sage to a cup of hot milk, particularly warming and enjoyable on a cold winter's day. Sage is also useful medicinally and cosmetically. A bunch of fresh sage leaves tied together and held under the hot tap when running a bath will wash the healing oils into the water and help give relief to rheumatic sufferers. A few sage leaves make an effective toothbrush – rubbed gently on the teeth, they will remove plaque, help clear stains and stimulate the gums.

SAGE TEA
This is not only a refreshing drink but acts as a general tonic and stimulant to the body, easing liver complaints, constipation, and the pain and stiffness of rheumatism. Pour 600 ml (1 pt) boiling water over 25 g (1 oz) of fresh sage leaves or 15 ml/1 tbsp dried and allow to stand for 5 minutes. Add a squeeze of lemon juice and a little honey if liked.

SAGE HAIR COLOURANT
An infusion of sage and China tea will help to restore the natural colour to hair that is turning grey.

5 ml (1 tsp) dried or 15 ml (1 tbsp) fresh sage
300 ml ($\frac{1}{2}$ pt) China tea
300 ml ($\frac{1}{2}$ pt) boiling water

Mix ingredients together and allow to steep for at least 2 hours. Strain, allow to cool and apply to newly shampooed, still damp hair with a brush or with the fingertips. It is advisable to wear rubber gloves and to take care not to stain the scalp or your hands and clothes. Reapply after six shampoos as the colour will gradually fade.

SAGE ASTRINGENT
Sage acts as a natural astringent and is beneficial to those with oily skins and open or damaged pores.

150 ml ($\frac{1}{4}$ pt) boiling water
30 ml (2 tbsp) chopped fresh sage
150 ml ($\frac{1}{4}$ pt) cider vinegar

Pour the boiling water over the sage and allow to stand until cool. Strain and add the vinegar. Keep in a screw-top jar or bottle and apply with cotton wool after first washing the face.

SAGE AND ONION SAUCE
This recipe is a tasty alternative to the more usual sage and onion stuffing and is particularly good with goose and turkey.

1 large onion, finely chopped
15 ml (1 tbsp) fresh sage leaves
60 ml (4 tbsp) water
30 ml (2 tbsp) fresh brown breadcrumbs
Salt and pepper
150 ml ($\frac{1}{4}$ pt) stock

Put the onion and sage in a saucepan with the water and simmer very gently for 10 minutes. Stir in the breadcrumbs and season with salt and pepper to taste. Add the stock and simmer for a further 5 minutes until thick. Cool before using.

SAGE RELISH
This is another delicious recipe which can be used on special occasions to flavour the gravy accompanying roast pork or chicken.

20 ml (4 tsp) fresh sage leaves or 10 ml (2 tsp) dried
10 ml (2 tsp) grated lemon peel
10 ml (2 tsp) salt
Pinch cayenne pepper
Pinch grated nutmeg
5 ml (1 tsp) lemon juice
400 ml ($\frac{2}{3}$ pt) red wine

Mix ingredients together and leave to stand, covered, for at least two weeks, shaking every day to mix thoroughly. Allow to clear and decant into screw-topped or corked bottle. Store in refrigerator.

SPARE RIBS WITH SAGE AND GINGER
(serves 4)

10 ml (2 tsp) dried sage, crushed
2.5 ml ($\frac{1}{2}$ tsp) ground ginger
2.5 ml ($\frac{1}{2}$ tsp) salt
Pepper
900 g (2 lb) pork spare ribs

Mix the sage, ginger, salt and pepper to taste together and rub them into the meat. Roast at 190°C/375°F (gas 5) on a rack above the roasting pan. Cook without basting. Serve with prawn crackers and gravy.

Borago officinalis

BORAGE

Family: Boraginaceae

'for the comfort of the heart, to drive away sorrow.'
– Gerard

Since Roman times borage has been famed as a cheerful plant, with a reputation for stimulating the mind and bringing courage. In the Middle Ages ladies would often embroider it on the scarves they gave to knights about to fight in tournaments or going off to the Crusades. As well as its medicinal and culinary uses, borage is a very attractive plant, favoured by botanical illustrators over the centuries, and included for its beauty in the garden at Versailles during the reign of Louis XIV.

Introduced to northern Europe by the Romans, borage now grows wild all over Europe and thrives on almost any wasteland. It is a grey-green hairy-leaved annual which grows as a perennial in mild climates. The bright blue, star-shaped flowers with dramatically contrasting black centres hang down in clusters from the thick stems and last for many months irrespective of the weather. Sometimes the plant will flower twice in one season and the brilliant blooms are a common sight on the rough land beside motorways. In good conditions the plant will grow to 60 cm (2 ft) high.

Cultivation

Borage will thrive provided the soil is well-drained and loamy and the position sunny. Grow from seeds sown in the early spring in drills about 4 cm ($1\frac{1}{2}$ in) deep and about 7.5 cm (3 in) apart. Sprinkle some dry lime on the soil, and you will have a fully grown plant in less than two months. If you have a strawberry patch, a few borage seeds sown there will help to stimulate the growth of both the strawberry and borage plants because the two are sympathetic to one another.

With its long tap root, borage is not particularly suitable for indoor growth and also does not take kindly to being transplanted. The leaves can be picked two months after the seeds are sown and dried for later use. Flowers can be picked as soon as they appear, which will also encourage the plant to continue blooming and prevent it seeding itself with otherwise gay abandon.

Uses

Borage makes a beautiful addition to a rockery and should be placed in a position in the garden where its lovely hanging flowers can be seen to advantage. Medicinally, borage is chiefly used today to relieve catarrh and colds and the headaches associated with them, although in the past it was also used as a general tonic. Make a hot infusion by adding 15 ml (1 tbsp) of finely chopped borage leaves to a cup of boiling water, allow to stand for 5–10 minutes before straining, and then drink.

Never dying Borage

Garden Borage

BORAGE FACE PACK

This is useful for those with dry skins. Make it by adding an egg yolk and 5 ml (1 tsp) of almond oil to a borage infusion, as described above. Add to a paste made with 7 g ($\frac{1}{4}$ oz) fresh yeast (or 5 ml/1 tsp dried) and a little water, and apply the mixture evenly to a clean dried skin. Leave for at least 10 minutes before rinsing off with cool water. Pat carefully with a soft towel.

Both the flowers and leaves of borage have a delicate cucumber flavour and can be eaten in salads or used to give a delicious flavour to soft cheeses and yoghurt. The flowers, which also look good dried and added to a pot-pourri, make particularly attractive crystallized decorations for cakes or desserts.

CRYSTALLISED BORAGE FLOWERS

Select newly opened flowers and pick as soon as the dew has dried from them. Place them on greaseproof paper and brush each flower carefully with a strong sugar syrup using a small paintbrush. Dust completely with sieved caster sugar and allow to dry at room temperature until hard. Store with the greaseproof paper in airtight jars.

HERB PUNCH

Borage is a traditional flavouring for Pimms No. 1 but for a cheaper, non-alcoholic alternative on a hot day, try this cooling herb punch.

30 ml (2 tbsp) lemon balm
30 ml (2 tbsp) borage
15 ml (1 tbsp) spearmint
1 litre (1$\frac{3}{4}$ pt) strong tea
Juice of 6 lemons
Juice of 2 oranges
170 ml (6 fl oz) fresh fruit juice (apple or pineapple)
Sugar syrup (1 cup sugar and $\frac{1}{2}$ cup water)
3 litres (5$\frac{1}{4}$ pt) ginger ale

Pour 1.7 litres (3 pt) boiling water over the lemon balm leaves and steep for 30 minutes. Strain into a bowl containing the borage and spearmint, and stir in the tea, fruit juices and syrup. Allow to stand for 8 hours or overnight. Strain and mix with the ginger ale, serve with plenty of ice and a large bunch of fresh mint.

White flowered Borage

Borago officinalis

Thymus vulgaris

THYME

Family: Labiatae

'The whole plant is fragrant, and yields an essential oil that is
very heating.'
– Culpeper

For centuries thyme has been a favourite herb. Its beautiful warm perfume lasts all year long, reminding us of summer even on the bleakest winter day, and its pretty clusters of purple flowers are a magnet to bees. Thyme-scented honey was one of the herb's greatest attractions to the Romans. They also valued the oil contained in thyme leaves for its antiseptic properties and used it as an antidote for headaches and depressions, as well as for incense to burn in their temples. They believed thyme to be a source of strength and in the Middle Ages, long after the Romans had introduced the herb to Britain, knights on their way to fight in the Crusades would wear a sprig of thyme as a symbol of strength and courage. Thyme, which is also said to be the herb of motherhood, makes an excellent rock garden plant and because of its strong fragrance, a distinctive flavouring in certain culinary dishes.

There are numerous varieties of thyme, some forming compact shrubs while others sprawl over the ground or spring from cracks in walls or between paving stones. When planted together, they tend to cross-pollinate and revert to the original type, wild thyme (*T. serpyllum*). This perennial plant grows all over Europe, preferring chalky or limestone soil and often spreading profusely on dry grassy banks. It is low-growing, with small evergreen leaves, and in summer the whole surface of the plant is a carpet of purplish flowers. Easily cultivated, it makes good ground cover and will trail prettily, giving off a strong scent if crushed or rubbed. Garden, or common, thyme (*T. vulgaris*) is equally an asset to the gardener. A hardy little shrub which requires almost no attention or feeding once established, it will brighten up any rockery or path.

Other varieties may not be as hardy but are well worth growing, particularly lemon thyme (*T. citriodorus*). As its name suggests, this has a lemon scent, useful in the kitchen, and its clusters of upright, deep pink, starry flowers are very popular with bees – honey made from lemon thyme has a delightful, subtle lemon tang. Some of the less hardy varieties also make pretty indoor pot plants, but it may be necessary to experiment to find out which are most suitable for your particular environment. Silver thyme (*T. vulgaris argenteus*) and the golden variety (*T. citriodorus aureus*), which has variegated leaves and a lemon scent, are both decorative but they will tend to revert back to green, especially if grown outdoors.

Cultivation

Thyme is a poor man's herb and does not appreciate a soil that is too rich or wet. If you have clay soil, add a few handfuls of lime chips and some peat before planting to lighten it and improve the drainage. Given a sunny position and good drainage, garden thyme will thrive through drought and downpour and grow to about 45 cm (18 in) high. If growing from seed, sow in the early spring in drills about 6 mm ($\frac{1}{4}$ in) deep and in the final flowering position, leaving a space of at least 30 cm (1 ft) wherever possible. Seeds pressed down between the cracks of flagstones will by autumn have grown into quite substantial little plants poking up from the path. After their first year of flowering clip back thyme bushes to prevent the woody stems from becoming sparse and straggly. Less hardy varieties like lemon thyme should be protected in winter from wet or freezing conditions with straw or cloches, otherwise there is a danger they will not survive until spring.

Thymus vulgaris

Marjoram Thyme

Great purple Wild Thyme

To propagate, either divide the roots of a well-established, mature plant in spring and replant, or in the early summer take cuttings from young shoots, which should be planted out in late spring. After about three years plants will start to go brown in the centre and die down, and it is therefore worth planting new each year in order to have replacements always available.

Thyme plants kept indoors must be given a sunny position or else they will shed their leaves. Never allow them to dry out between waterings or to become water-logged, and once the young plant grows, clip it back to encourage a bushy growth.

Uses

Thyme has valuable antiseptic properties and an infusion of the herb applied to the skin will help relieve insect bites, clear spots and act as a soothing skin tonic. Made into a herbal tea, it will help relieve headaches and ease throat and chest infections, and the dried leaves and flowers make a delightfully fragrant addition to a pot-pourri or herb cushion. Sprigs of thyme, fresh or dried (and securely tied in a muslin bag), can be added to the bathwater for a refreshing, perfumed bath, and the herb is no less valuable in the kitchen. It is an essential ingredient of bouquet garni but because of its strong taste, it should always be used sparingly. A sprig or two added to casseroles and stews, soups and sauces, or placed on top of roast lamb or pork before cooking, will bring out the flavour of the meat. The more delicate lemon thyme can be used to replace lemon rind or, finely chopped, can be sprinkled on salads or added to the nutmeg on baked custards.

SKIN TONIC

Take 5 ml (1 tsp) of dried thyme leaves and flowers, or 15 ml (1 tbsp) of fresh thyme, and add 200 ml ($\frac{1}{3}$ pt) boiling water. Allow to stand for 30 minutes, then strain. Apply to the face with cotton wool, or pour into a warm bath, and it will soothe and soften the skin and help relieve skin irritations. The tonic will stay fresh for several days if stored in a sealed bottle in the refrigerator.

THYME TEA

Pour 600 ml (1 pt) boiling water over 10 ml (2 tsp) of dried thyme, or 20 ml (4 tsp) of fresh thyme, which has been bruised or coarsely chopped. Allow to stand for about 10 minutes. Honey can be added as a sweetener. This herbal tea will relieve headaches brought on by tension, overtiredness, working in a smoky atmosphere, or other minor reasons, and because of its antiseptic properties it will also ease sore throats, colds and chest infections.

SOLE WITH BÉCHAMEL SAUCE (serves 4)

Thyme is particularly good in béchamel sauce to bring out the flavour of what could otherwise be rather bland white fish.

4 medium-sized sole
900 ml (1½ pt) milk
4 sprigs fresh thyme
1 bay leaf
Salt and white pepper
4 shallots, finely chopped
4 sticks of celery, finely chopped
30 ml (2 tbsp) flour
Grated nutmeg

Wash the fish and dry carefully. Bring half of the milk to boil. Place the sole in sauté pan and season with salt and pepper. Add thyme and bay leaf and cover with the boiling milk. Cook at 180°C/350°F (gas 4) for 30 minutes. Remove from oven and place fish on a warm dish, reserving the juices. Melt the butter in a saucepan, add finely chopped shallots and celery and cook until shallots are transparent. Remove from heat, stir in flour and cook for 1 minute. Gradually add the remaining milk and juices from the sole, stirring continuously until smooth. Simmer gently for 15 minutes, remove sprigs of thyme and bay leaf and pour over sole. Sprinkle with grated nutmeg and serve immediately.

TOMATO AND CHEESE QUICHE WITH THYME (serves 2)

225 g (8 oz) shortcrust pastry
25 g (1 oz) butter
1 small onion, finely chopped
75 g (3 oz) strong cheese, grated
2 firm tomatoes (sliced)
2 firm tomatoes, sliced ·
150 ml (¼ pt) milk
15 ml (1 tbsp) fresh thyme leaves, finely chopped, or 7.5 ml (1½ tsp) dried
Salt and pepper

Roll out the pastry thinly and line an 18 cm (7 in) flan tin. Prick well and bake blind for 15 minutes at 200°C/400°F (gas 6). Sauté the onion in butter until transparent. Fill the base of the partially baked flan case with the onion and grated cheese. Whisk the eggs with the milk and pour through a strainer on to the onion and cheese and top with the tomatoes. Season with thyme, salt and pepper. Return to oven and bake for a further 15 minutes or until filling is set.

Lemon Thyme

Hoary Wild Thyme

Mentha pulegium

PENNYROYAL

Family: Labiatae

'Pennyroyal taken with honey cleanseth the lungs and
cleareth the breath from all grosse and thick humours.'
– John Gerard

Pennyroyal, one of the many varieties of mint, was christened by the Romans *mentha pulegium* or 'flea mint' and for many centuries this strongly scented herb was used to repel insects. Sailors in the sixteenth century used it to purify their water supply, and it was also used medicinally as a remedy for jaundice, dropsy and coughs, including whooping cough in children. In the north of England pennyroyal is popularly known as 'pudding grass' because it is a traditional flavouring in the popular black pudding.

The plant makes excellent ground cover – in less than six months this little creeping perennial can cover an area of about 90 cm (3 ft) and, unless checked, it will form a dense evergreen carpet around other plants. Its small, oval leaves are an attractive shade of dark green, contrasting pleasantly with the reddish-brown stems which from July to October bear tiny whorls of lilac flowers. These flower-bearing stems can reach 15 cm (6 in) in height during the growing season. The whole plant emits a delicious minty perfume when walked on.

Cultivation
Like all mints, pennyroyal is very easy to grow but in common with other herbs it prefers a light, well-drained soil. Propagate in the spring and autumn by lifting young shoots, each with its cascade of tiny white fibrous roots hanging from it, separate them from the parent plant and replant with a light covering of soil. Plant these cuttings at least 15 cm (6 in) apart, otherwise they will soon choke each other, and keep these young plants moist at all times. The tiny roots will soon form another plant and since the centre of the old plants die out, it is wise to have young ones ready to replace them.

Pennyroyal is an excellent plant for container growing either indoors or outside and it will thrive in a window-box. It will even tolerate strong sunlight but the soil must always be kept moist. If the plant is clipped back it will not grow too tall and will make an attractive evergreen pot plant with a delightful fragrance.

Uses
Because it repels insects, pennyroyal is useful in the garden for deterring ants and grown indoors it will help keep flies away. If ants are a problem in the larder, try rubbing a few leaves on the shelves and in the corners where they are particularly attracted. Some crushed pennyroyal leaves added to unscented cold cream or ointment makes an effective insect repellant rubbed on to exposed skin – a useful tip for campers – and if there is no cream or ointment available, try rubbing the leaves directly on to the skin. A few crushed leaves sprinkled into bedding will also help safeguard the sleeper from fleas and bugs, and – more applicable nowadays – will help keep domestic animals free of insect pests that they are likely to pick up in the warmer weather. If this does not prove effective, try rubbing the animal's coat with a few crushed pennyroyal leaves.

The herb is also useful medicinally and in the kitchen, where it makes a pleasant alternative garnish to the more usual garden mint for new potatoes, peas and young carrots. It is, however, stronger in flavour and should be used more sparingly.

PENNYROYAL TEA
This has a strong minty flavour and tastes particularly

good with a slice of lemon and a little honey. It also acts as an anti-depressant and will ease a persistent cough if taken regularly. Make it in the usual way, with about one heaped teaspoon (5 ml) of dried leaves or a tablespoon (15 ml) of fresh leaves to one cup of boiling water, leaving it to steep for about five minutes.

PENNYROYAL BUTTER
This savoury butter is delicious dotted on roast lamb or fresh young vegetables.

75 g (3 oz) butter
15 ml (1 tbsp) chopped pennyroyal leaves
7.5 ml (1½ tsp) lemon juice
Salt and black pepper

Soften the butter in a bowl, then mix in the pennyroyal and gradually add the lemon juice. Season with salt and pepper and beat until smooth. Form into small balls or shapes and chill or freeze until needed.

PENNYROYAL SORBET (serves 4)
As with most sorbets this can be prepared well in advance and kept in the freezer until required. It makes a refreshing dessert on hot summer days.

75 g (3 oz) caster sugar
300 ml (½ pt) water
4 sprigs pennyroyal
Juice of 1 large lemon (about 45 ml/3 tbsp)
1 egg white
Tiny sprigs of pennyroyal for decoration

Place sugar and water in a pan, bring to the boil and boil for 2 minutes. Wash the pennyroyal carefully and pat dry. Stir into the pan, then remove pan from the heat and allow to stand for 30 minutes. Strain into a container and add the lemon juice. Place the container in the freezer for about an hour until the mixture is almost frozen. Meanwhile beat the egg white until stiff. Fold it into the half-frozen mixture and return the container to the freezer. Half an hour before the sorbet is due to be served, remove the container from the freezer to allow the mixture to thaw slightly, then spoon into individual serving dishes and decorate with a small sprig of pennyroyal.

PENNYROYAL STUFFING
This is particularly good as a stuffing for rolled shoulder of lamb or roast mutton.

60 ml (4 tbsp) finely chopped onion
50 g (2 oz) butter or margarine
40 g (1½ oz) fresh breadcrumbs
45 ml (3 tbsp) chopped parsley
450 ml (¾ pt) chopped fresh pennyroyal
15 ml (1 tbsp) sugar
Salt and pepper

Fry the onion in a little of the butter or margarine until transparent. Add the remaining fat and when melted, mix in the breadcrumbs, parsley, pennyroyal and sugar. Season with salt and pepper. Allow to cool before using.

Pennyroyal

Ruta graveolens

RUE

Family: Rutaceae

'For the malady called lethargy, which is forgetfulness,
take the herb rue, rinse it in vinegar and lay it on the brow.'
– Unknown writer, sixth century BC

The botanical name for rue is derived from the Greek word *rhyesthai*, to save or help, and for many centuries this attractive herb has benefited humanity. In Roman times it was used extensively as an antidote to poison, particularly snake bites, and it was the Romans who introduced rue to Britain and elsewhere in Europe as a cure for poisoning. It was long revered as a holy plant – the Druids would strew it in their homes and places of worship to ward off the devil and evil spirits, and later, during the Plague, rue was kept in the home to protect the inhabitants from plague-carrying fleas. The floors of jails and court-rooms were also strewn liberally with rue to keep at bay the dreaded jail fever, carried by rat fleas, and even up to the end of the last century judges and court officials would sometimes carry a small bunch of rue as protection against infection from the prisoners.

The herb was also used as an ingredient in herb wine during the Middle Ages and is still used in Spain and southern Italy to give aroma to brandy. Today, however, rue is used more as a decorative plant than for its medicinal and culinary powers. Its lacy blue-green leaves are evergreen, a great point in its favour, and it is very easy to grow. The compact and shrubby perennial will reach a height of about 60 cm (2 ft) and in summer the mass of leaves is topped with greenish-yellow flowers which are followed by green lobed capsules and seeds.

Cultivation

Rue needs sun but will grow in the poorest of soils. It can be propagated by dividing the mature plant, taking cuttings or from seed. Rue seeds are slow to germinate and should be sown in the spring in a light, well-drained limey soil. Transplant them to their permanent position when the seedlings are large enough to handle. Cuttings can be taken from a mature plant in the late summer, kept in a cold frame during the winter and planted out in the spring; or propagate by lifting and dividing the root of a mature plant in the autumn and replanting directly in the flowering position.

Take care when handling rue plants because they can produce a painful rash similar to nettle rash and it is advisable to wear gloves, particularly if you have a sensitive skin. The plants will last for several years and will keep their bushiness if the flower heads are pinched out each year.

With its delicate leaves and unusual flowers, rue makes an attractive houseplant, although even given the sunniest position you may find that it is reluctant to bloom indoors. A well-lit spot is essential – artificial light will be helpful when there is no sunshine – and plant the seeds or cuttings in a well-drained light soil. Keep the soil moist at all times or the plant will become thin and sparse, and do not fertilize more than once a month. Clip back the taller shoots to encourage a neat, compact shape.

Uses

Insects dislike the smell of rue so an indoor plant is helpful in keeping a room free of ants and flies, and a few dried rue leaves scattered on the soil around an insect-plagued plant will help to clear the problem. A strong infusion made by pouring a little boiling water on dried or fresh rue leaves can be dabbed on insect bites to bring relief and a weak tea made from rue leaves can be sipped or used cold as an eye-wash to ease eye strain. It is the ingredient called rutin

Ruta graveolens

Wild Rue with white flowers

contained in the herb which is believed to help the eyesight and during the Renaissance rue was often used by craftsmen and artists whose livelihood depended on good vision. Because of its rather bitter flavour, rue should be used sparingly in the kitchen but it is a useful herb in some dishes and acts as a general stimulant to the appetite.

RUE VINEGAR
Rue leaves added to vinegar will give it extra flavour.

300 ml ($\frac{1}{2}$ pt) white wine or cider vinegar
3 fresh rue leaves
Pinch coriander seeds

Mix the ingredients in a screw-top bottle and place on a sunny ledge, shaking the bottle every day for three weeks, by which time the vinegar will have taken up the flavour of the rue.

ROAST PHEASANT WITH RUE (serves 4)
1 large pheasant, dressed plus giblets
2 rashers bacon
sprig fresh thyme or 2.5 ml ($\frac{1}{2}$ tsp) dried
15 ml (1 tbsp) flour
3 fresh or 2 dried and crushed leaves rue

Wash and dry the bird thoroughly and place in roasting pan with bacon covering the breast to prevent it drying out. Sprinkle with chopped thyme and roast for 30 minutes at 200°C/400°F (gas 6). Take bird from oven and remove bacon. Dredge with flour, baste, sprinkle with rue and return to oven for 30 minutes until crisp and brown. Use giblets for gravy and serve with bread sauce.

COTTAGE CHEESE WITH RUE

A pinch of dried rue helps to lift the mild flavour of cottage or cream cheese.

150 g (5 oz) carton cottage cheese (unflavoured)
15 ml (1 tbsp) double cream
Pinch salt
Pinch dried rue

Soften the cheese with the cream and stir in the salt and rue. For added flavour prepare the day before use and refrigerate. This is delicious served on rye bread or toast as a snack.

Garden Rue

Monardo didyma

BERGAMOT

Family: Labiatae

This sweet scented herb is a native of North America where its benefits had been recognized by the Oswego Indians long before bergamot was introduced to Europe in the sixteenth century. They were probably the first to make the soothing and mildly antiseptic tea known as Oswego tea, which patriotic Americans are supposed to have drunk after the Boston Tea Party in 1773 when tea from Britain was boycotted, and in North America the herb is still named after them.

Bergamot is a tall perennial plant which in summer will grow to 90 cm (3 ft) in height. It is a member of the mint family and has both the minty flavour of common mint which makes it useful in the kitchen and a similar appearance, except for its spectacular scarlet flowers which appear in nettle-shaped clusters in late summer. Bees are greatly attracted to it but so unfortunately are caterpillars and grasshoppers and the plant may have to be sprayed if they become a problem.

Cultivation

Bergamot prefers to grow in partial shade and will flourish on a rich moist soil. An ideal situation for it is in the shade of some tall shrubs whose fallen leaves will not only protect the young plants from frost but will also provide humus for the coming year. Propagate from cuttings in the spring or autumn, taking pieces of stem about 10 cm (4 in) long with a little heel to them. Dip them in a rooting compound and plant in a light soil, keeping them moist at all times until they are well-established, when they can be transplanted to their permanent position. Towards the end of the flowering season, the stems of bergamot tend to become brittle and the plant will need to be staked and tied in to prevent the flowers being blown down in windy weather and the plant's shape being ruined. Bergamot will die down in the autumn and winter and it may be necessary to mark its position with a stick. After a few years, the centre of a large plant will begin to die out and look brown and ugly so it is also worth propagating by digging up a mature plant and dividing the roots to make smaller plants.

Bergamot can be grown successfully in a container providing it is kept moist, and it makes an attractive and useful addition to a patio or small town garden.

Uses

A herb cushion made with bergamot and such herbs as lemon balm, lavender and peppermint will not only smell sweet but will ease headaches caused by nervous strain and help induce sleep. Bergamot, like all mints, contains the antiseptic thymol and drinks made from it will benefit those suffering from sore throats as well as acting as a general relaxant. A few dried bergamot flowers and leaves can also be added to China or Indian tea and even to wine for a similar soothing effect.

OSWEGO TEA

Take 5 ml (1 tsp) of dried bergamot flowers to one cup of boiling water and simmer gently for 5 to 6 minutes. The result will be a clear, wine-coloured tea, which can be sweetened with honey if necessary.

BERGAMOT MILK

Pour 300 ml ($\frac{1}{2}$ pt) of hot milk over 15 ml (1 tbsp) of dried bergamot leaves and allow to stand for a few minutes. Strain and drink while still hot.

SAVOURY TENDERLOIN OF PORK (serves 4)
Bergamot is particularly delicious when added to pork dishes.

900 g (2 lb) Spanish onions
10 ml (2 tsp) chopped bergamot
Salt and black pepper
15 g ($\frac{1}{2}$ oz) flour
4 pork chops from the spare rib, or tenderloin
15 ml (1 tbsp) chopped gherkins (optional)

Dice onions and mix with bergamot – add 5 ml (1 tsp) salt and pinch black pepper. Put in casserole with 150 ml ($\frac{1}{4}$ pt) water (or cider if available). Grill the pork chops for about 10 minutes on each side. Place in casserole with onions and juices and cook for a further 45 minutes at 180°C/350°F (gas 4). Remove the chops and onions, and skim off the fat. Stir flour into remaining stock and return to oven to brown. Add the onions and browned stock and reheat. Serve the chops with this onion gravy. Garnish with chopped gherkins if liked.

ORANGE AND BERGAMOT SALAD
(serves 4 to 6 as a side dish)
The minty taste of bergamot will give a refreshing lift to an orange salad.

Take 4 oranges, peel and remove all pith. Chop coarsely and pile into a small bowl. Cover with chopped or bruised bergamot leaves and stir well. Leave for an hour to absorb juices, then serve on a bed of lettuce or watercress with an oil and vinegar dressing.

POTATOES AND BACON WITH BERGAMOT (serves 4)

125 g (4 oz) diced bacon
50 g (2 oz) butter

10 small onions or shallots
15 ml (1 tbsp) flour
300 ml ($\frac{1}{2}$ pt) stock
700 g (1$\frac{1}{2}$ lb) cubed potatoes
10 ml (2 tsp) bergamot

Fry the bacon in the butter, add the onions and cook until transparent. Remove the bacon and onions. Stir the flour into the fat in the pan until brown. Add stock and bring to boil. Put the potatoes into this sauce with the bacon and onions. Bring to boil, cove and cook at 130°C/250°F (gas $\frac{1}{2}$) for 1 hr. Serve sprinkled with chopped bergamot.

BERGAMOT COTTAGE CHEESE

5 ml (1 tsp) lemon juice
1 litre (2 pt) milk
5 ml (1 tsp) salt
5 ml (1 tsp) chopped bergamot leaves

Add lemon juice to the milk, stir thoroughly, then cover and leave until the milk is thick and sour. Add bergamot leaves, tip into muslin and leave to drain over night.

BERGAMOT JELLY

3 handfuls of chopped bergamot leaves
1.8 kg (4 lb) cooking apples
350 g (12 oz) white sugar per 600 ml (1 pt) juice

Peel and slice the apples and put in a large pan with enough water to cover and the bergamot leaves. Simmer until soft, then pour into a clean jelly bag. Leave to drip through overnight.

Measure the juice and add the sugar. Stir over a low heat to dissolve the sugar, then bring to a rolling boil. Boil for 8 minutes before testing for setting point. Put a little of the jelly on a cold plate and if a skin forms quickly the jelly is ready. Pour into warm, clean jars, seal and cover.

Monardo didyma

Lavendula officinalis

LAVENDER

Family: Labiatae

'The decoction of the husks and flowers drunke, openeth
the stoppings of the liver, the lungs, the mitt, the mother,
the bladder and in one worde all other inward parts,
clensing and driving forth all evill and corrupt humours,
and procureth urine.'
– John Gerard

This popular sweet-scented herb is a native of the warm limestone hills of the Mediterranean coastal region and it was frequently used by the Romans to perfume their bathwater – its name comes from the Latin word *lavare*, to wash. Lavender was treasured in Elizabethan England, where lavender bushes often formed the low hedges surrounding flower beds in Tudor knot gardens, and when a little later the Pilgrim Fathers sailed to North America, they made sure to take lavender with them. It was used to give fragrance to clothing and to repel moths at the same time, and then as now, the blossoms were made into perfume. Fields of lavender can be seen today in France and central Europe and in the English counties of Norfolk and Surrey, where the herb is cultivated for the perfume industry. Lavender leaves were used extensively in cooking in the past but the herb is now probably more valued for its fragrant, pain-soothing qualities.

There are many varieties of this attractive, perennial shrub, some tall, some dwarf, with flowers that range from dark to light purple and even to white. All have grey leaves, for lavender, like sage bushes and olive trees, belongs to a plant type called xerophytes – plants which have adapted to living in dry conditions and have leaves that retain moisture. One of the most common varieties is *Lavendula officinalis* or English lavender which is very like *L. vera* or Old English lavender and is low-growing with spikes of deep mauve flowers. *L dentata* or French lavender, also a common variety, will grow into a large bush and has pale mauve flowers. These are all hardy plants but some varieties, such as Italian lavender, are fragile.

Cultivation

Ideally lavender needs a light, dry limestone soil but it will thrive on London clay and if this is your type of soil, give it a top dressing of peat in the autumn. The plant needs a sunny, uncrowded position, sheltered from severe frosts and high winds. Although lavender can be propagated from seed or division

Common Lavender

Lavendula officinalis

of the roots, cuttings are the easiest and most successful method. Take 10 cm (4 in) cuttings of young stem with a heel from a mature plant in the summer. Dip these in rooting powder and plant in sand. Keep the cuttings in a greenhouse or in the shelter of a south-facing wall and plant them out in the following spring when they should be well-rooted. Allow a minimum space of 60 cm (2 ft) between plants if you are growing French lavender or another large variety; smaller varieties will only need 30 cm (12 in) to 40 cm (16 in) spreading room. If you are planting a lavender hedge, English or French lavender is most effective but should you also be aiming to have a range of flower colours, remember to plant varieties that will grow to a uniform size or the hedge will appear uneven and patchy.

Lavender also makes an ideal indoor plant. In colder, northern climates *L. dentate* is a good variety to choose because it adapts happily to indoor growing and will form a compact bush that does not need to be pruned and releases its perfume spontaneously as soon as it is touched. For indoor growing, plant a well-rooted cutting in potting compost containing lime chips. Keep the soil on the dry side but do not allow it to dry out completely; if in doubt water as soon as the plant shows any sign of flagging and then let the soil dry before watering again. Pot-grown lavender needs plenty of air space so do not crowd it in with other plants or it will refuse to flower.

Uses

The beautiful fragrance of lavender makes it an essential ingredient in a herb pillow or pot-pourri; also try adding a few heads of lavender to the sugar container for deliciously scented sugar. The herb has the power to calm the nerves and to relieve headaches and faintness. Frozen lavender sticks are sold commercially for this purpose but it is easy to make your own pain-soother by adding 15 ml (1 tbsp) of crushed lavender flowers to a cup of boiling water and when the infusion is cool, applying it as a cold compress to the temples and forehead. Lavender oil, apart from its delightful fragrance, acts as a powerful antiseptic and was used to dress wounds in the Second World War when commercial sterilizers were in short supply. The herb is not often used in the kitchen but a blossom or a few leaf spikes added to soups and stews will give them a definite spiciness;

always use lavender sparingly as a culinary herb, however, because both the flowers and leaves have a hot flavour.

LAVENDER OIL

This soothing antiseptic oil will help ease aching rheumatic joints and it also makes an effective insect repellant – rub on to exposed skin before taking a summer walk or when camping.

400 ml ($\frac{2}{3}$ pt) almond oil or green olive oil
Large handful of crushed lavender flowers
15 ml (1 tbsp) white wine vinegar

Put all the ingredients in a screw-topped 0.5 litre (1 pt) bottle and shake vigorously. Leave the bottle on a sunny windowsill for about 2 weeks, shaking well every day. Test that it is ready for use by rubbing a little on the skin and seeing if the perfume lasts for a few minutes; if not, keep up the process for another few days.

LAVENDER VINEGAR

Fill a screw-topped 0.5 litre (1 pt) bottle almost to the brim with white vinegar and add six heads of lavender. Leave on a sunny windowsill for at least 2 weeks. Use this sweetly scented vinegar for salad dressings and savoury dishes.

CHICKEN CASSEROLE WITH LAVENDER
(serves 4)

4 portions of roasting chicken
60 ml (4 tbsp) oil
4 leaves of lavender
5 ml (1 tsp) dried basil
5 ml (1 tsp) salt and a pinch of black pepper
30 ml (2 tbsp) tomato purée
$\frac{1}{2}$ bottle of dry white wine

Wash and carefully dry the chicken pieces. Heat the oil in a casserole and brown the chicken on all sides. Mix the lavender, basil, salt and pepper together and sprinkle over the chicken. Add the tomato purée and pour in the wine. Place a lid on the casserole and cook at 180°C/350°F (gas 4) for 1$\frac{1}{2}$ hours or until tender.

BAY

Family: Lauraceae

'Neither witch nor devil, thunder nor lightning, will hurt
man where a bay tree is.'
– Culpeper

The aromatic bay is a native of the Mediterranean area and its leaves were used by the ancient Greeks and Romans to crown their warriors and literary heroes. It is traditionally believed to be a protection against the Devil and to promote the general health and happiness of mankind. Because of its scent and antiseptic qualities, it was used as a strewing herb, and its natural oils are an ingredient in many old medical recipes. Today it is more valued in cooking and as an attractive addition to the patio and garden.

Bay is in fact a tree, although it is classed as a herb, and will grow up to 12 metres (40 ft). A hardy perennial evergreen, it has shiny smooth leaves similar to laurel – being a member of the same family – and in spring it bears small yellow flowers which are followed by purple fruits in the autumn if the weather has been mild.

Cultivation

Bay is not particular about the soil in which it grows but it will need shelter from severe winds and harsh weather. The most successful and easiest way to grow it is to buy a young established plant from a nursery, however, these tend to be expensive and the alternative is to take young shoots from an established plant in the late summer or from hardwood in the autumn. Plant these in a container and be prepared to bring them under cover at the first sign of frosts or they may die. Plant out the following spring or grow in large tubs either indoors or out, where they can be formed into ornamental shapes. Encourage compactness by snipping off any lateral branches or suckers in the autumn so that the topmost shoots are encouraged and a standard tree on a central stem will be formed.

Bay leaves can be picked all the year round and

used either fresh or dried. Pick them mid-morning after the dew has gone and use the same day or dry them in an airy place in full sunlight for at least 2 weeks before storing in airtight jars.

Bay tree

Wild Bay tree

Uses

The oil in bay leaves contains healing properties which will bring relief to aching limbs and muscles, particularly if this is caused by excessive exercise or exertion.

BAY OIL

50 g (2 oz) bay leaves, crushed
300 ml ($\frac{1}{2}$ pt) pure olive oil
15 ml (1 tbsp) white wine vinegar

Place the ingredients in a screw-top jar and leave in a warm place, ideally on a sunny windowsill, for 2 weeks. Shake the mixture each day and after 2 weeks when the bay will have released its healing properties into the oil, strain and add some fresh bay leaves. Leave for a further 4 weeks, after which time the oil will be ready for use.

Bay is the only form of laurel to be used in cooking. It is one of the essential herbs used in 'bouquet garni' and can be used for flavouring meats, gravies, beef stock, casseroles and soups.

BOUQUET GARNI

1 bay leaf
5 ml (1 tsp) dried parsley
5 ml (1 tsp) dried thyme
10 ml (2 tsp) lovage
5 ml (1 tsp) dried marjoram
1.25 ml ($\frac{1}{4}$ tsp) dried sage

Mix all the ingredients and tie them into little muslin bags. Remember to remove before serving!

LENTIL SOUP WITH BAY (serves 4)

125 g (4 oz) red lentils
850 ml ($1\frac{1}{2}$ pt) chicken stock
2 onions, chopped
125 g (4 oz) spinach, chopped
2 sprigs parsley
Sprig of sage
1 bay leaf

Pick over the lentils and remove any grit. Rinse, then place in a pan and cover with the chicken stock. Bring to boil and simmer for 30 minutes. Add onions and chopped spinach and simmer for a further 15 minutes. Add herbs, and continue to cook slowly for a further 20 minutes. Remove bay leaf and sage and purée the soup for a few minutes in a blender. Serve immediately with croûtons.

RICE AND TREACLE PUDDING WITH BAY
(serves 4)

Bay can also enhance the flavour of puddings and sweets. Try it in this recipe for a delicious winter dessert.

30 ml (2 tbsp) pudding rice
15 ml (1 tbsp) golden syrup or black treacle
600 ml (1 pint) milk
1 bay leaf
Knob butter

Blend together the rice and syrup in an ovenproof dish and gradually add scalded milk. Add bay leaf and knob of butter and bake in a cool oven, 130°C/250°F (gas $\frac{1}{2}$), for $1\frac{1}{2}$–2 hours.

Laurus nobilis

FENNEL

Family: Umbelliferae

'The Green leaves of Fennel eaten do fill womens breasts
with milk.'
– John Gerard

Fennel has been used as a culinary herb for many centuries and was known to the ancient civilizations of China, India and Egypt. The Spanish are recorded as growing it commercially in the tenth century and in the Middle Ages it was often used for medicinal and cosmetic purposes. Sprigs of fennel hung over the threshold of the door at midsummer were an ancient insurance policy against evil spirits entering the home for the rest of the year. Fennel was also one of the herbs strewn over the carpetless floors of our ancestors to keep their homes sweet-smelling and free from infection.

A tall, feathery perennial, fennel is one of the most beautiful plants in the herb garden. Whatever the season there always seem to be a few bright green ferny leaves on show and in summer it is majestic, surrounded by its distinctive aniseed scent and lovely umbels of yellow florets. These appear in July and last right through until October and the first frost, attracting bees and swallow-tailed butterflies.

Cultivation

Fennel grows easily among rocks and in sandy dry soils. It thrives on sunshine and particularly in a well-drained calcium-rich soil, where it will not require extra feeding. Grow from seeds, planted in the autumn for harvesting the following year. Allow a minimum of 45 cm (18 in) between each plant to to allow it to spread, and avoid growing it near dill, coriander and angelica because the plants tend to cross-pollinate and thus lose their individual flavours. Harvest the seeds when they have turned brown; if you leave them, the plant will seed itself and you may find fennel plants growing all over the garden and appearing in chinks in walls and cracks in paving stones.

Uses

There are many medicinal and cosmetic uses for fennel, apart from its culinary powers. Make an infusion by soaking 5 ml (1 tsp) of fennel seeds in water for about 10 minutes, then adding 15 ml (1 tbsp) of fresh leaves which have been pounded using a pestle and mortar, and pour over a cup of boiling water. Strain and sip to help relieve cramp pains. An infusion made in the same way but using just the leaves can be used to ease tired or watery eyes by applying cotton-wool pads soaked in the mixture. Alternatively, make a poultice by crushing the leaves and adding a little grated raw potato to them; spread the mixture on to a piece of muslin or cheesecloth, and hold the poultice on the eyelids for about 15 minutes. Rinse well with cold water and dry carefully with a clean cloth. Always use fresh fennel for these remedies and use the infusions within 12 hours; they do not store even if kept in the refrigerator.

CLEANSING LOTION
This recipe is particularly beneficial to those suffering from an oily skin. It is also reputed to prevent wrinkles!

30 ml (2 tbsp) crushed fennel leaves
300 ml ($\frac{1}{2}$ pt) boiling water
150 g (5 oz) carton live natural yoghurt

Pour the boiling water on to the fennel leaves to make

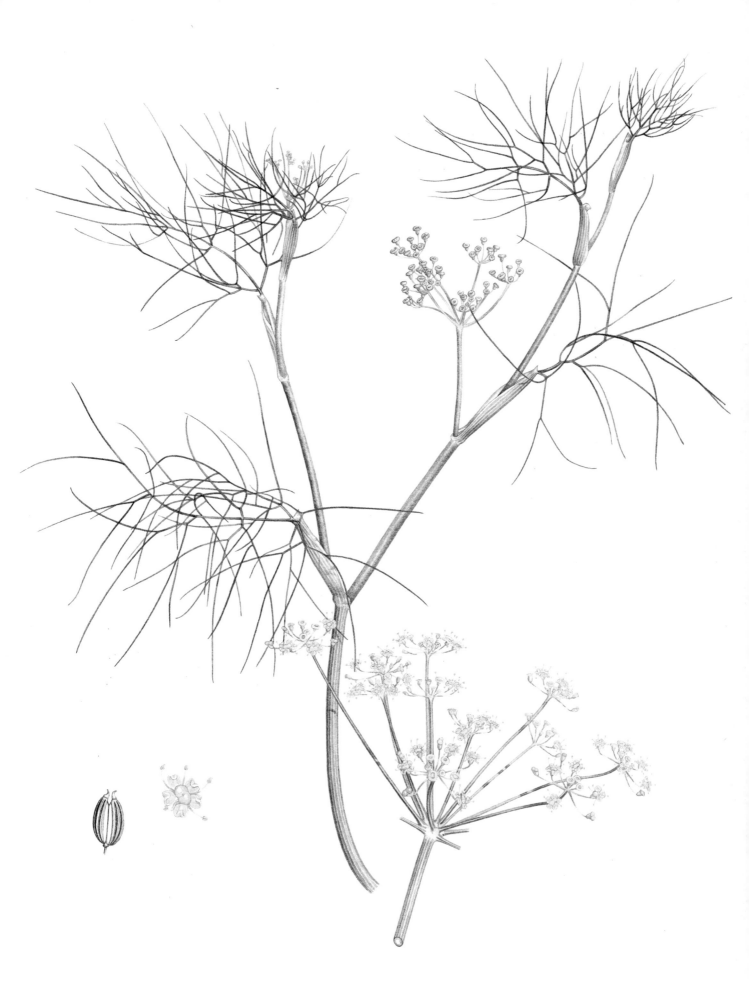

Foeniculum vulgare

a strong infusion. Leave to cool, strain and then stir in the yoghurt until well blended. Massage gently into the skin and rinse off with cold water, patting the skin dry with a clean towel. The skin will feel softer as well as cleansed. Any surplus lotion can be kept for a few days if stored in the refrigerator.

GRIPE WATER
For babies or anyone suffering from wind or general stomach upsets, this will help bring relief.

15 g ($\frac{1}{2}$ oz) fennel
15 g ($\frac{1}{2}$ oz) common mallow
15 g ($\frac{1}{2}$ oz) young nettles
7 g ($\frac{1}{4}$ oz) feverfew
300 ml ($\frac{1}{2}$ pt) boiling water

Crush all the leaves, place in a jug and pour the boiling water over them. Allow the mixture to steep for 10 minutes, then strain and sip while still warm.

Fennel's aromatic, bitter-sweet flavour makes it very useful in the kitchen. It is popularly called the slimmer's herb because the seeds can be chewed to keep hunger pangs at bay, and it is also a general aid to digestion, particularly of fatty foods.

FENNEL STUFFING
This is an excellent accompaniment to mackerel or eel, or other rather greasy foods, where fennel helps to counteract the fattiness.

25 g (1 oz) butter
1 small onion, chopped
50 g (2 oz) brown breadcrumbs
Salt and freshly ground black pepper
30 ml (2 tbsp) chopped fresh fennel leaves
1 egg

Melt the butter in a frying pan and sauté the onion until transparent. Stir in the breadcrumbs and add salt and pepper to taste. Add chopped fennel and stir in the beaten egg. Mix well, leave for 5 minutes before using.

JACKET POTATOES WITH FENNEL
Fennel is delicious when added to jacket potatoes, particularly if these accompany fish or roast pork.

4 medium-sized potatoes
Butter as required
4 sticks 5 cm (2 in) each of dried fennel stalk

Scrub the potatoes and make a small hole in each with a sharp knife. Fill the hole with butter and push in a piece of fennel. Place on the oven shelf and bake at 200°C/400°F (gas 6) until the potatoes begin to soften (about 35 minutes). Remove from the oven and push the fennel stalks further into the potatoes. Continue to cook until the potatoes are soft (15 minutes more). Serve with the stalks still inside and pass extra butter.

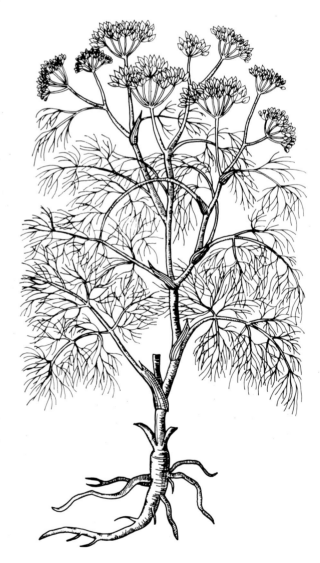

Common Fennel

Nepeta cataria

CATMINT

Family: Labiatae

'Cats will rub themselves upon it, wallow and tumble in it
and also feed upon the branches and leaves very greedily.'
– Gerard

True catmint (*Nepeta cataria*) is a deliciously perfumed herb, native to Britain, which has been used medicinally since the eighteenth century and which was also used to mask the smell of meat that had been salted or cool-stored over the winter. It should not be confused with garden catmint (*N. mussinii*), which does not contain the medical properties of true catmint and grows in a different way. All varieties have a strong mint scent which attracts not only cats but insects such as caterpillars and grasshoppers which enjoy breakfasting on the young plant. Once established, however, catmint will survive these poachers and renew itself after attacks or being rolled on.

Catmint is a short, medium-sized perennial with heart-shaped, gently toothed leaves which are covered with a soft greyish down. In June the nettle-shaped florets appear in mauve whorls around the leafy stems and in good conditions they will last through until September, making a thick, spreading carpet of soft green and mauve around other plants. Garden catmint is more densely growing than true catmint, which can often be seen growing wild in hedgerows and waysides, and therefore it makes a better rockery or edging plant, even though it lacks the medicinal qualities of true catmint. It also make a good indoor pot plant because it will not spread as rampantly.

Cultivation

Grow catmint from its tiny seeds which should be sown in the late autumn in a light, sandy soil and preferably in a sunny position. Allow plenty of space for the plant to spread and once the seedlings appear, keep a watch for cats and insects; if necessary, cover them with a cloche until they are well established.

If growing catmint indoors, plant the seeds in a potting compost enriched with lime, keep them moderately damp and fertilize with a well-balanced fertilizer. Keep the pot in a light position, preferably

Nep or Catmint

Small Catmint

Great Catmint

sunlight but fluorescent light will do almost as well, and once the seedlings have established themselves, keep them well-trimmed so that the woolly leaves thicken out.

Uses

True catmint makes a natural, non-addictive mild sedative which is particularly useful for children who are unable to settle down at night. Use a few crushed dried leaves, add a cup of boiling water and allow to stand until cool, then strain. If taken hot, this tea will also help bring down a high temperature during a fever.

Cat lovers can also use this herb to make a toy for their pet by cutting out two pieces of firm material, possibly in the shape of a ball or mouse, sowing them firmly round the edges but leaving a gap at one side, then turning the shape inside out. Dried catmint can then be used to stuff the shape, and the remaining edge sewn up, with a piece of string attached so that the toy can be pulled along. Resist the temptation to add beads and buttons for eyes or nylon bristles for whiskers because they can be dangerous if they become detached.

Catmint – the true variety – also has its uses in the kitchen, where the minty flavour will benefit bland dishes or vegetables such as marrows or courgettes.

COURGETTES WITH CATMINT (serves 4)

450 g (1 lb) courgettes
50 g (2 oz) butter
15 g ($\frac{1}{2}$ oz) fresh catmint, finely chopped

Wash the courgettes and remove the ends. Slice and sauté in butter in a heavy frying pan. Season, then cover and simmer until tender, ensuring that both sides are properly cooked. Before serving, sprinkle with catmint.

GRAPEFRUIT AND CATMINT DESSERT
(serves 4)

2 medium grapefruit
125 g (4 oz) caster sugar
5 ml (1 tsp) fresh catmint, chopped
850 ml (1$\frac{1}{2}$ pt) cold water

Peel off the grapefruit rind very thinly, taking care to avoid the white pith. Put into a blender. Remove pith and discard. Coarsely chop the grapefruit flesh and add to the blender with the caster sugar, catmint leaves and cold water. Blend until the mixture is light green. Strain into stemmed glasses and refrigerate until well chilled. Garnish with a redcurrant leaf or a sprig of catmint.

Nepeta cataria

HYSSOP

Family : Labiatae

'Made with figs, water, honey and rue and dandelion, helpeth
the inflamation of the lungs.'
– John Gerard

Hyssop is thought to have originated in southern Europe and from there to have spread to the Middle East where it was used for medicinal purposes many years before the time of Christ. Both the Old and New Testaments of the Bible mention hyssop, which lepers used to rub on to their skins in an effort to cleanse themselves of their disease and to protect those they met from being infected. Its antibiotic properties were also valued by agricultural workers; a poultice made from the bruised leaves mixed with sugar would be applied to cuts and bruises incurred whilst working in the fields in order to ward off the possibility of tetanus and to reduce swelling. The herb is perhaps more valued now for its strong fragrance, which makes it useful in the perfume industry – it is one of the ingredients in eau-de-Cologne – and in the kitchen. In the past it was used to preserve meat and it continues today to be part of the secret of the delicious liqueur Chartreuse. Its sweet scent is a powerful attraction to bees, and in the monastic gardens of the Middle Ages hyssop was often grown near fruit trees to encourage pollination. Hedges of hyssop around fruit trees are equally useful today, although since they will also attract butterflies, it is wise not to grow green vegetables near them if the Cabbage White is not to be lured into the vicinity.

Hyssop is a medium-sized hardy perennial and its flowers are an asset to any garden. They bloom from July through to September in violet-blue whorls which form a long spike of colour along the weedy stems. Although a native of warmer climes, it will tolerate colder weather and can occasionally be found growing wild both in Britain and North America.

Cultivation
Hyssop is fairly undemanding about soil conditions but prefers a sunny position. It can be propagated by seeds or division of the roots. If using seeds, plant in the spring on well-drained, chalky soil and fertilize

Dwarf narrow leafed Hyssop

Hyssopus officinalis

Hyssop with blue flowers

Hyssop with reddish flowers

well with lime. They germinate very quickly and should start to be visible within a week of planting. Once the seedlings are large enough to be handled, transplant them into an open bed. To propagate by splitting a mature plant, make sure the soil is thoroughly moistened and loose, then lift the roots, prizing them apart gently by using two garden forks placed back to back. This technique will cause far less damage than chopping at the roots with a spade. When young plants are about 45 cm (18 in) high, cut them back to encourage new tender leaves.

Hyssop is an ideal, shrubby herb for growing in a container either outside or inside on a sunny window-ledge. Use a 12 cm (5 in) pot containing light, well-drained, chalky soil and plant the seeds shallowly, keeping the soil moist. Trim the plant regularly and it will form an attractively shaped bush.

If leaves are to be dried, they should be cut shortly before the plant begins to flower when they have the greatest concentration of natural oils.

Uses

The dried leaves and flowers make a particularly fragrant addition to a pot-pourri or, tied in a muslin bag, to the bathwater. Apart from being an attractive and useful garden plant – the roots help purify the surrounding soil – hyssop can be used medicinally and in cooking. A mild infusion of the leaves will help ease the pain and discoloration of a black eye; apply it directly with an eyebath or soaked in muslin or cotton wool. If crushed stems of the herbs are added to this infusion and it is applied as a poultice as hot as is bearable, it will help bring a stye to a head and reduce inflammation. This infusion can also be used cold to dab on insect bites and stings to bring relief.

COUGH SYRUP

Make a strong infusion by adding one cup of boiling water to 10 ml (2 tsp) of bruised leaves and leave to stand for about 10 minutes. Strain and add a little honey for sweetness. This is particularly beneficial to the lungs and chest, and will ease a persistent ticklish cough and the heaviness of catarrh.

The delicate minty flavour of hyssop makes the herb useful in many culinary dishes, savoury and sweet. A few leaves can be added to salads, and to stews and casseroles, and are particularly good with game,

White flowered Hyssop

Thin leafed Hyssop

rabbit or lamb. They can also be added to stewed fruit, such as cranberries or peaches, or served with them in pies and flans. The refreshing tang of hyssop makes it an ideal addition to fruit cups.

LAMB RAGOUT WITH HYSSOP (serves 4)

50 g (2 oz) lard
1.4 kg (3 lb) middle neck of lamb, chopped
2 large onions, chopped
60 ml (4 tbsp) flour
Grated nutmeg
Salt and pepper
600 ml (1 pt) beef stock
1 clove
30 ml (2 tbsp) lemon juice
15 ml (1 tbsp) hyssop leaves or 2 small sprigs

Heat the lard in a heavy casserole and fry meat until sealed. Add onions and fry till beginning to brown. Sprinkle sifted flour, nutmeg and salt and pepper over meat, and add beef stock, clove and lemon juice. Bring to boil. Add hyssop leaves tied in a muslin bag, or sprigs, cover casserole and transfer to oven. Cook

for 2 hours at 180°C/350°F (gas 4). Remove hyssop leaves or sprigs and serve with creamed potatoes or plain boiled rice.

PARTRIDGE PIE WITH HYSSOP

225 g (8 oz) lean pork
Salt and freshly ground black pepper
15 ml (1 tbsp) hyssop leaves
1 young partridge
125 g (4 oz) bacon, diced
150 ml ($\frac{1}{4}$ pt) beef stock
Shortcrust pastry to cover
1 egg yolk

Finely mince the pork and season with salt and pepper. Add finely chopped hyssop leaves. Divide the partridge into serving portions and place in a pie dish lined with half the minced pork mixture. Add the bacon and the rest of the minced pork. Moisten with beef stock and cover with shortcrust pastry. Glaze with brushed yolk of egg and bake in a moderate oven, 190°C/375°F (gas 5) for $1\frac{1}{2}$ hours until golden.

Taraxacum officinale

DANDELION

Family: Compositae

'Boiled in vinegar it is good against the pains that trouble
some in making water.'
– John Gerard

The often maligned dandelion is a plant that is entirely beneficial to us. Its botanical name comes from the Greek 'taraxis', meaning 'disorder', and 'akas', meaning 'remedy', and dandelions have many healing powers that have been valued for centuries. Arab physicians of the past used them as a general tonic and stomachic, and dandelions frequently appear in the medical recipes of the Middle Ages. They do, however, act as a stimulant to the bladder, which has earned them the French nickname 'pissen-lit' (wet-a-bed). The plant's high vitamin and iron content makes it a health-giving food, and the ethylene gas which it gives out encourages fruit crops to ripen more quickly – some farmers deliberately encourage dandelions to grow under their trees to ensure an early harvest. Dandelions also rot down readily on the compost heap and the soil nutrients that have been absorbed by the long tap root can be fed back to be appreciated by more shallow-rooted plants.

Dandelions, despite all their valuable properties, are often considered a pest because of their ease of propagation, and most gardeners will find them growing somewhere in their lawns. They are a native of Eurasia and now grow all over the northern hemisphere. The plant is a short, low-growing perennial with hollow flowering stems, sometimes tinged with red, which are smooth and shiny and full of a milky juice that seeps out if the stem is broken. Each stalk produces an individual, bright yellow daisy-like flower with outer florets whose underside is purplish-grey. The flowers appear all the year round but particularly between April and June. The fleshy leaves are broadly toothed and formed in a rosette; the plant's English name derives from the French

'dent-de-lion' (lion tooth) which refers to the shape of the leaves – like the backward-slanting teeth of a lion.

Dandelions not only have the ability to reproduce from fragments of root that are left in the soil but their abundant seeds have adapted themselves brilliantly to germination. The wind disperses the tiny parachutes of the dandelion 'clock', which can travel for many miles; in dry weather the minute hairs forming the parachute will spread out to enable the seeds to fly and in rain or damp they will close so that the seeds are dropped on to wet soil.

Cultivation

Dandelions will thrive in any soil and any climate other than the extremely hot. Sow seeds thinly at any time from early spring to the end of summer, keep the bed well-watered and do not allow the soil to dry out. Once the plants have started to grow, pick off any flowering stems to encourage leaf growth. As the plants are perennials, they should last for many years, but do not cut too many leaves during the first year or you will sap the plant's strength.

Uses

There are many medicinal uses for dandelions. A dandelion tea taken regularly will aid the digestion and is reputed to ease rheumatism and relieve the kidneys and liver of stones and poisons. Dandelion juice gently massaged on to stiff joints caused by un-accustomed exercise should relieve the ache, as will dandelion tea.

A strong infusion of dandelion (1 litre/1¾ pints)

Taraxacum officinale

added to the bathwater will generally tone and freshen the skin, and is particularly beneficial after months of winter sluggishness. Or, for the same effect, tie a muslin bag full of crushed dandelion leaves to the hot water tap and let the goodness of the herb be washed into the bathwater.

SKIN TONIC

This will revitalize tired skin and generally improve the circulation. Make it by crushing 5 ml (1 tsp) of fresh dandelion leaves and adding a cupful of boiling water. Leave to infuse for about half an hour, strain and use when cool. The tonic can be stored in a sealed bottle in the refrigerator for about 10 days without losing its power.

Because of their nutrients, dandelion leaves are very useful in the kitchen – in France they are sold on market stalls as an alternative to lettuce and other salad greens. They are especially useful for a salad early on in the year when lettuces are scarce and expensive, and make an excellent vitamin-rich tonic after the long winter months. The taste is more bitter than lettuce so use the leaves sparingly.

SPRING SALAD

Chop young dandelion leaves, nasturtium, chives and cress, cover with a dressing made from equal measures of tarragon vinegar and olive oil seasoned with salt and freshly ground black pepper, and toss well before serving.

DANDELION GREENS

Cooked dandelions make a tasty vegetable that is even more beneficial than spinach.
Thoroughly wash dandelion leaves and cook in boiling water for 5 minutes. Drain and discard the water. Cook leaves in fresh, salted boiling water for a further 10 minutes, strain and serve with butter. As a variation mix in a little cream and garnish with chopped hard-boiled egg.

DANDELION COFFEE

Dandelion roots may be dried, ground and roasted as a substitute for coffee and although lacking the

stimulant that caffeine gives, the taste is very good. Dig up the plant in the autumn. Wash and dry it and put in a cool oven 110°C/225°F (gas $\frac{1}{4}$) until crisp. Roast when needed, grind and use as coffee.

DANDELION WINE

Dandelion wine has an interesting, delicate flavour. Always pick the dandelions on a warm sunny morning. Shake out any insects and remove the flower heads completely from the stalks, together with the green calyx that is formed under the sepals.

2.2 litres (4 pt) dandelion petals
2.2 litres (4 pt) boiling water
Rind of 1 lemon, thinly pared
Rind of 1 orange, thinly pared
1 cm ($\frac{1}{2}$ in) root ginger
Juice of half a lemon
7.5 ml (1$\frac{1}{2}$ tsp) wine yeast and nutrient
900 g (2 lb) loaf sugar (or clear honey)
Campden tablets

Put the dandelion petals in a large bowl and pour over the boiling water. Allow to stand for 3 days stirring frequently. Strain into a preserving pan. Add the lemon and orange rind, ginger and lemon juice. Gently simmer for half an hour. When cool add yeast and sugar and allow to ferment in a warm place for 4 to 5 days. As the yeast grows the 'must' will become creamy in colour. At this stage transfer to a fermentation jar fitted with a fixed air lock. Fermentation will take about 6 weeks after which time the wine may be filtered through a siphon into a sterilized container. Take care not to include any of the sediment when siphoning as this will make the wine bitter. Once the wine is thoroughly filtered, crush one campden tablet per 5.7 litres (10 pt) of wine to stop fermentation from continuing. Store in a cool dry place. Filter the wine every two months until it becomes clear after which it can be poured into sterile bottles, corked and labelled.

Ocimum basilicum

BASIL

Family : Labiatae

'The juice clenseth away the dimness of the eyes and drieth up
the humour that falleth into them.'
– John Gerard

This ancient herb, possibly the oldest of all the herbs, originated from India where it is still commonly grown today and used for its culinary powers and also as an antidote to venemous snake bites. Basil probably spread to Europe via the Middle East and it was famed as a herb with extraordinary powers. Its name comes from the Greek 'basileus' meaning king, and the ancient Greeks and Romans and the Jewish people used it to give strength during times of fasting. It is also known as the herb of poverty, protecting the needy and destitute.

There are two main varieties of basil, sweet basil (*Ocimum basilicum*) and bush basil (*O. minimum*). Both are annuals, at least in cool climates, and both have a delicious peppery flavour invaluable in cooking. Sweet basil has large, dark green, shiny leaves and can grow to about 60 cm (2 ft) high, producing a profusion of small white flowers in the late spring. Bush basil grows into a compact shape, rarely more than 15 cm (6 in) high, with similar leaves and flowers. There is a hybrid variety, opal basil, which has dark, purply-green leaves and pale pink flowers.

Cultivation
The larger sweet basil is more suitable for outdoor growing and likes a sheltered position and light, dry, well-drained soil. Grow from fresh dry seed – if you notice a smoky-blue jelly appearing on the seeds, it means they have become damp in storage. Wait until all danger of frost has passed before sowing and do not over-water or the seeds will rot.

The small and compact bush basil is ideal for growing indoors in a pot, and there are other strains which will also grow well indoors, such as French valmorin basil, which has a particularly delicious flavour and is distinguished by its light green leaves, and the lemon-scented basils originating from Egypt which are similar to the French variety but with toothed leaves. Grow from seed in a small pot (6 cm/2½ in maximum) filled with rich soil that has a plentiful supply of lime. Ensure that the drainage is good and the soil moist at all times or else the plant will shed its leaves. If kept in a warm, light position, basil is one of the easiest herbs to keep indoors and not only is useful in the kitchen but looks very attractive.

Uses
Basil's main use is in cooking but it does have other uses. Indoor basil plants have long been used by the French, Italians and Greeks to keep away flies, and medicinally it is very useful for those who suffer from travel sickness. One teaspoon (5 ml) of the dried herb or 1 tablespoon (15 ml) of fresh to one cup of boiling water, left to stand for a few minutes, then strained, can be sipped before embarking on a journey and will calm the stomach. This infusion is also very effective if sipped when cold and is particularly useful for pregnant women suffering from morning or all-day sickness, because there is no fear of affecting the unborn child as there is with drugs.

OIL OF BASIL
This oil, massaged into the temples, will relieve nervous tension and headaches.

400 ml (⅔ pt) almond oil or green olive oil
15 ml (1 tbsp) wine vinegar
Handful of fresh basil

Mix the ingredients in a sealable jar or bottle and leave to stand in a sunny position for 2 weeks, shaking the jar each day. Strain and return the liquid to the jar with a fresh handful of basil. Leave to stand for a further 4 weeks, strain and use.

All forms of basil are useful in the kitchen but the herb has a strong flavour and should be used sparingly and, to avoid bitterness, not left to cook for long periods. Fresh leaves are preferable – they are best if picked as soon as they unfurl and before the plant has flowered. Leaves for drying can be picked at the end of the summer when the plant is cut down; they may take longer to dry than those of other herbs and as an alternative they can be salted by layering them in a pottery container – layer of salt, layer of leaves, etc – and then sealing the container with a cork.

(Remember to rinse off the salt thoroughly before using.) The freshly cut stems can also be dipped in olive oil which will act as a preservative.

BAKED TOMATOES WITH BASIL (serves 4–6)
Basil is a natural accompaniment to tomatoes, enhancing their tangy flavour.

75 g (3 oz) butter
2 Spanish onions, thinly sliced
900 g (2 lb) skinned tomatoes, sliced
30 ml (2 tbsp) fresh basil, chopped
50 g (2 oz) fresh breadcrumbs
Sea salt and freshly ground black pepper

Great Basil

Citron Basil

Preheat the oven to 200°C/400°F (gas 6). Grease a medium-sized baking dish. Melt about a third of the butter in a frying pan and sauté the onions until transparent. Beginning with the onions, make layers in the baking dish of onions and tomatoes sprinkled with basil, then scatter the breadcrumbs over the top and dot with the remaining butter. Season with salt and pepper. Bake in the oven until the top is browned, which should take about 30 minutes.

CREAMED HADDOCK SOUP WITH BASIL
(serves 4)

700 g (1½ lb) fresh haddock
2 small onions
4 sprigs basil
4 sprigs parsley
300 ml (½ pt) water
50 g (2 oz) butter
50 g (2 oz) flour
300 ml (½ pt) milk
Tomato to garnish
Sea salt and freshly ground black pepper

Place the haddock in a pan, add most of the onions and the basil and parsley, and cover with water. Bring to the boil and simmer gently until just soft. Remove the fish, reserving the stock, and flake finely, removing any bones. Melt the butter in a pan and stir in the flour to make a smooth paste. Cool for 1 minute. Add the milk and bring gently to the boil, stirring continuously. Add 300 ml (½ pt) of the reserved stock and continue to stir over gentle heat until the sauce is smooth. Season to taste. Remove from heat and add the fish. Serve garnished with the remaining onion and slices of fresh tomato.

PIZZA ALLA NAPOLETANA (serves 4)
Bread dough

15 g (½ oz) fresh yeast or 10 ml (2 tsp) dried
300 ml (½ pt) lukewarm water
450 g (1 lb) flour
5 ml (1 tsp) salt
30 ml (2 tbsp) oil

Cream the yeast with a little of the water, cover and leave in a warm place until frothy. If using dried yeast, add 5 ml (1 tsp) of sugar. Sift the flour into a bowl,

Bush Basil

with the salt add yeast liquid and remaining water. Mix to a soft dough with the oil. Knead until smooth and elastic on a floured surface. Place the dought in a floured bowl and cover with a damp cloth. Leave in a warm place until doubled in size (about 2 hours). Knead dough again and divide into two. Roll out to make two pizza bases. Place on greased baking trays, brush with oil and add filling.

Filling

450 g (1 lb) tomatoes, skinned and sliced
6 anchovy fillets
50 g (2 oz) black olives
225 g (8 oz) Mozzarella cheese
60 ml (4 tbsp) olive oil
Salt and pepper to taste
5 ml (1 tsp) basil
2 cloves of garlic
5 ml (1 tsp) oregano

Grease two 18 cm (7 in) flan tins and line with dough. Cover dough with a layer of tomatoes, then top with anchovies and olives. Season to taste. Grate cheese and sprinkle over the mixture. Pour over a dressing made of the olive oil, oregano, basil and crushed garlic. Bake in a fairly hot oven, 200°C/400°F (gas 6), for 30 minutes until cheese is bubbling.

COMFREY

Family: Boraginaceae

'The slimie substance of the roote made into a posset of ale,
and given to drink agaynst the paine in the back, gotten by any
violent motion as wrestling . . . , doth in fower or five daies
perfectly cure the same, although the involuntarie flowing
of the seed in men be gotten thereby.'
– Gerard

Commonly called 'bone-set' or 'knit-bone', comfrey has been used medicinally for over two thousand years. Its name comes from the Latin 'confirmare', to unite, and the herb was indispensable in the past for the healing of fractures and wounds. Comfrey would always be found in the monastery gardens of the Middle Ages, when tending to the sick and injured was one of the monks' traditional duties, and so famous were the legends about this miraculous herb that it was even added to bathwater to restore lost virginity! The healing substance which it contains is called allantoin, which helps the body to replace cells after an injury or operation and also helps to protect it from minor illness.

Comfrey is a perennial plant belonging to the borage and forget-me-not family and grows abundantly in damp places during the summer months. It favours fenlands and the banks of streams and brooks, and can often be found growing in clumps in the shade of deciduous woods. Full and leafy with stout branching stems and fleshy leaves covered with soft hairs, it grows vigorously and at maturity will reach 60–90 cm (2–3 ft) in height. Its bell-shaped flowers vary from creamy white to purple and appear in forked, thick, one-sided clusters from late spring onwards. The variety known as Russian comfrey is sometimes used by farmers as cattle fodder and has blue flowers with leaves that tend to be covered in coarse hair; it prefers a drier soil and can frequently be seen growing on wasteland and by the roadside.

Cultivation

Provided a severe drought does not occur, comfrey will survive and multiply with very little attention. Choose a moist and fairly sunny position in the garden where it will not swamp other plants when it grows and prepare the soil by digging it deeply. Propagation is best achieved by lifting and dividing the root clumps of a mature plant in late summer or by removing some of the outside roots. The root pieces, which should be about 7.5 cm (3 in) long, can be planted straight into the ground or potted for planting out the following spring. Cover the root pieces with about 2.5 cm (1 in) of fine soil and keep moist. The new plants should begin to appear in about a week if the weather is warm.

Uses

Comfrey is particularly useful to the gardener because it will enrich the soil and is invaluable on the compost heap, where its abundant leaves will help break down the waste matter quickly and organically. As a shortcut, the fresh leaves can be buried in the vegetable garden (before the flowers have seeded) so that their high nitrogen content is released into the soil rapidly. The leaves can also be used to make a quick-acting feed for flagging tomatoes: soak comfrey leaves in water, using about two to three times the quantity of water to leaves, and allow to stand for a few days. The potash produced can be applied directly to the tomato plants and any left over will be appreciated by marrows and courgettes. The decomposing leaves can be added to the compost heap so that nothing is wasted.

The long-searching roots of comfrey are equally useful in the garden. Not only do they break up the soil so that natural minerals from the subsoil are brought to the surface, but they contain a concentrated supply of the healing allantoin which is so useful medicinally.

Symphytum officinale

Comfrey

Comfrey's most famous medicinal power is the healing of broken bones but the same healing attribute applies to many lesser complaints. Its haemolytic action helps to dissolve clots of red blood corpuscles and therefore reduces bruising and swellings from knocks and falls. Make an ointment by taking freshly grated comfrey root and mixing it to a smooth paste with a little water; apply it to the affected place and cover with a clean bandage. This has a remarkably soothing effect and can also be used to ease burns and scalds. To heal smaller cuts and grazes, make an infusion of fresh comfrey leaves and boiling water and apply with pads of cotton wool.

COMFREY TEA

This will soothe an upset stomach and because of comfrey's powers to stimulate tissue replacement will be particularly beneficial to those with stomach ulcers. It will also relieve coughs and inflammation of the lungs, and help cure diarrhoea and gastroenteritis. Make it by adding 25 g (1 oz) of dried comfrey leaves to 600 ml (1 pt) of boiling water; leave to stand, then strain and allow to go cold. Sip frequently.

SKIN TREATMENT

Not only will this restore the skin's freshness and thoroughly cleanse the pores without overstimulating greasy skin, but it has the beneficial side-effect of relieving laryngitis, catarrh and smoker's cough. First, clean the face and neck with a non-greasy cleanser or cleansing milk, rinsing several times afterwards with tepid water, and patting the skin dry. Put 60 ml (4 tbsp) of finely chopped fresh comfrey leaves in a large bowl and pour on 1.1 litres (2 pt) boiling water. Lean well over the bowl, taking care not to touch the water and cover the head with a towel so that all the steam is trapped. If possible, remain in this position for 10 minutes. Rinse the face gently with tepid water and, if you wish, also use a mild skin toner. Pat dry.

Comfrey also has its uses in the kitchen where the leaves, finely chopped, can be prepared as a green salad or a few can be added to a mixed salad to make a subtle change. The leaves are well-stocked with iron and calcium, as well as iodine and vitamins A, B and C, so the salad will be particularly beneficial.

FRESH COMFREY SALAD WITH CRESS

1 crisp lettuce
125 g (4 oz) finely chopped comfrey leaves
1 punnet mustard and cress
30 ml (2 tbsp) tarragon vinegar
90 ml (6 tbsp) olive oil
1 clove garlic, finely chopped
10 ml (2 tsp) French mustard
Lemon juice
Salt and freshly ground black pepper

Wash and dry the lettuce carefully. Arrange the smaller leaves around the outside of the salad bowl. Shred the larger leaves and mix with comfrey and mustard and cress. Place in salad bowl. Mix vinegar, oil, garlic, mustard and lemon juice thoroughly and pour over salad. Season with salt and pepper. This salad is delicious served with fresh made bread and cottage cheese.

COMFREY FRITTERS

Wash and dry a handful of young comfrey leaves. Dip in batter (as used for pancakes) and deep fry quickly. The little leaves will turn up in the hot oil and emerge like tiny fried green fish. They can be used as an unusual starter for a dinner party.

Allium schoenoprasum

CHIVES

Family: Liliaceae

'They cause troublesome dreams.'
– John Gerard

Chives are one of the most useful culinary herbs in the garden – a few snippings will enhance the flavour of almost any savoury dish. They are also one of the most ancient of all herbs and are included in Chinese herbals as long ago as 3000 BC, although they were not introduced to Europe until the sixteenth century. Apart from their delicious flavour, chives are very nutritional, containing iron and pectin, and they also act as a mild antibiotic.

One of the onion group of plants which includes garlic, chives are a hardy perennial and resemble tiny onions. The mini bulbs grow together in clumps and the leaves are hollow and grass-like; the more the leaves are snipped, the thicker the plant will become. In spring and early summer the small, pompom-shaped flowers appear as a delicate mauve. They are very attractive but unless the plant is being grown for ornamental reasons, the flowers should be removed if the flavour of the leaves is to be retained. Chives will grow to about 38 cm (15 in) in the summer but will die right back in winter. It is advisable to mark their positions with a stick or stake if they are not to be disturbed by winter digging.

Cultivation

Chives are very easy to grow and will tolerate most conditions, although they flourish best on rich soil that contains plenty of humus. They tend to use up large quantities of nitrogen and potassium, and if these are not replaced, the leaves will turn yellow. Some of the nutrients they remove from the soil can however, be easily replaced by emptying tea leaves and coffee grounds on to the chive bed. Choose a warm position in the garden but preferably out of direct sunshine, and either sow seeds in the early spring, thinning the seedlings out as soon as they are large enough to handle, or propagate by dividing an already established clump. Since seeds are slow to germinate, the latter is the much easier method, and if necessary you can buy a small pot of chives and plant them – they will multiply quickly provided they are kept moist.

Several clumps of chives are better than one because they can then be split up in rotation. When propagating by division, it is a good idea to keep a few chives in a pot which can be brought indoors in the late autumn to provide a winter supply for the kitchen. If kept moist and fed every few weeks, they will survive happily on the kitchen windowsill without the leaves turning brown. If the leaves stop growing, allow the plant to dry out completely, then place it in the refrigerator for about a month. If it is then returned to a warm position and sparsely watered, the leaves should start to grow again. If this does not work, repeat the process. And if the plant becomes too large, turn it out of the pot, divide the roots and repot.

Drying chive leaves is not, unfortunately, very successful because they tend to turn brown and change flavour, but before the winter frosts set in the last leaves can be picked and quick-frozen.

Uses

Chives are said to stimulate the appetite and also to relieve high blood pressure. A few crushed chive bulbs added to boiling water, then allowed to cool, can help ease a troublesome cough if the drink is sipped regularly. Their main use, however, is in the kitchen where their subtle onion flavour is an invaluable addition to salads, soups and cheese and egg dishes. They will also help to counteract the fattiness of some foods and thereby aid digestion.

BAKED COTTAGE CHEESE WITH CHIVES (serves 4)

Chives are particularly good for adding flavour to cottage cheese.

450 g (1 lb) tomatoes
450 g (1 lb) cottage cheese
30 ml (2 tbsp) Worcestershire sauce
30 ml (2 tbsp) chopped chives

Preheat the oven to 200°C/400°F (gas 6). Remove the skins and seeds from the tomatoes and chop the flesh. Mix with the cottage cheese, Worcestershire sauce and chopped chives. Place in an ovenproof dish and bake for 20 minutes. Serve immediately.

TOMATO SOUP WITH CHIVES (serves 4)

1 Spanish onion
50 g (2 oz) butter
700 g (1½ lb) ripe tomatoes
600 ml (1 pt) chicken stock
5 ml (1 tsp) sugar
Pinch sea salt and freshly ground black pepper
30 ml (2 tbsp) chopped chives

Peel and chop the onion finely. Melt the butter in a saucepan and gently cook the onion until transparent. Skin the tomatoes, remove the seeds, and add the chopped flesh to the onion. Stir. Heat the chicken stock and pour into the saucepan. Season with salt and pepper and add the sugar. Bring to boil and simmer for 15 minutes. Allow to cool then purée in a blender. Chill the soup thoroughly and stir in the chopped chives before serving.

EGG AND CHIVE SALAD (serves 6)

6 hard-boiled eggs
1 small can salmon or tuna fish
90 ml (6 tbsp) mayonnaise
30 ml (2 tbsp) chopped chives

15 ml (1 tbsp) dry white wine
Salt and black pepper
Oil and vinegar dressing
1 crisp lettuce

Shell the eggs, then halve lengthways and remove yolks. Mash fish to a smooth paste and add to egg yolks. Stir in mayonnaise, chives and wine. Season with salt and pepper. Fill the eggs and chill thoroughly. Serve on bed of crisp lettuce leaves with oil and vinegar dressing.

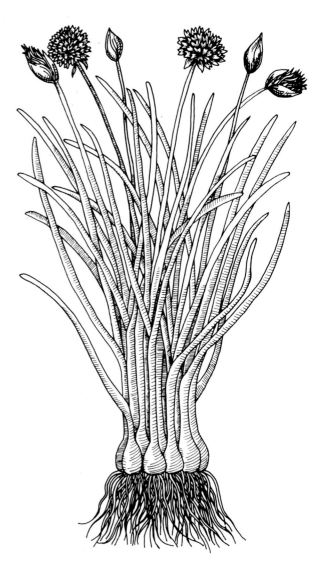

Chives

Allium schoenoprasum

Anthriscus cerefolium

CHERVIL

Family: Umbelliferae

'Wholesome for the feeble stomache.'
– Gerard

Chervil is another of the herbs brought to Britain by the Romans, and because of its allegedly cleansing properties it was traditionally eaten during the Lenten fast. The plant has a tangy, slightly sweet flavour rather like parsley and is beloved by French cooks. In appearance it is also similar to parsley. It is a small, annual herb with fern-like leaves and, if kept well-trimmed, makes a compact bushy plant that is as decorative indoors and out. Once established outdoors, the flowering stems will reach a height of about 45 cm (18 in) in the summer and will bear tiny white florets. Chervil is one of the few herbs that grows more readily indoors than out and is particularly worth cultivating because it is difficult to buy in shops, becoming limp and bedraggled within a short time of being picked.

Cultivation

There are two types of chervil, curly and plain, and both will seed themselves freely once they are established, but it takes care to achieve an established plant. Young plants do not transplant easily and it is best to grow chervil from seed. Make sure the seeds are fresh – chervil seeds do not keep for long – and ideally find a place in the garden which provides dappled light and shade, such as underneath a deciduous tree where the plants will have shade during the summer and protection from frost by falling leaves in the winter. Sow the seeds in the spring directly into the flowering position and about 25 cm (10 in) apart. Cover each seed lightly with about 2 cm ($\frac{3}{4}$ in) of potting compost and keep moist until the seeds have germinated. They germinate very quickly and with regular planting through the spring and early summer you should be able to maintain a supply of fresh leaves throughout the year, since chervil will remain green for the whole of the winter if the climate is not too cold. However, it is wiser, especially as chervil grows well inside, to make sure of a winter supply by planting some seeds in small pots for growing under glass or in a window-box. Use a mixture of light sandy potting compost and keep the soil moist; the plants should be ready for cutting within about six weeks. Be careful if you are growing chervil on a sunny windowsill because it will only tolerate full sunlight if the atmosphere is cool, so in a warm kitchen you will need to put a fan on regularly if the plant is to survive.

Incidentally, chervil does not dry or freeze well, and its leaves should never be picked by pulling them from the plant because there is a danger that the whole plant will be uprooted, so snip them off with scissors or use a sharp knife. If an outdoor plant is not being grown for its seeds but its leaves, remember to nip off the flowers.

Uses

Chervil is invaluable as a flavouring in many dishes but it also has some medicinal and cosmetic uses. A strong infusion of chervil will ease gnat and mosquito bites, dabbed on the affected area at regular intervals, and a particularly good cleansing lotion can be made very simply with chervil leaves.

CLEANSING LOTION

This is especially helpful to those with greasy skins or sufferers from spots and acne. Take a 150 g (5 oz) carton of natural yoghurt and mix it with an infusion of chervil, made by pouring 150 ml ($\frac{1}{4}$ pt) boiling water

Common Chervil

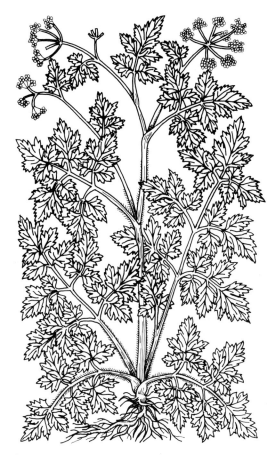

Hedge Chervil

over at least 30 ml (2 tbsp) of fresh chervil leaves, and allowing it to stand until cool before straining. Wash the face carefully before applying and rinse off thoroughly with tepid water. The cleanser can be kept for up to a week if stored in a screw-top bottle in the refrigerator. The effect will be particularly beneficial if the cleansing is followed by a final application of a mild chervil infusion, dabbed on to the skin with cotton-wool. This too can be kept for up to a week in the refrigerator without losing its freshness.

Chervil is one of the chief ingredients of 'fines herbes' and the finely chopped leaves make a delicious garnish for soups, particularly cold consommé, and for many other savoury dishes, hot and cold.

OMELETTE AUX FINES HERBES (serves 2)

4 eggs
salt and pepper
15 g ($\frac{1}{2}$ oz) butter
30 ml (2 tbsp) mixed fresh chopped chervil, parsley, chives and tarragon

Break the eggs into a bowl and season with salt and pepper. Gradually melt the butter in an omelette pan until the base of the pan is coated evenly. Beat the eggs and add to the pan all at once. As the eggs begin to set, gently stir so that the liquid mixture runs under the set eggs and the omelette is cooked evenly. Add the chopped fresh parsley, chervil, tarragon and chives and fold the omelette over. Add a knob of butter to the omelette and garnish with any remaining herbs. Serve immediately.

STUFFED EGGS WITH CHERVIL
(serves 6 as a starter)
Chervil is a natural accompaniment to egg dishes, and particularly good with stuffed eggs.

6 hard-boiled eggs
150 ml ($\frac{1}{4}$ pt) single cream
Salt and pepper
4 sprigs chervil
50 g (2 oz) butter
45 ml (3 tbsp) plain flour
150 ml ($\frac{1}{4}$ pt) milk

Great Chervil or Myrrh

Small Sweet Chervil

Cut eggs in half lengthways. Remove yolks, blend them with a tablespoon of the cream and season with salt and pepper. Finely chop the chervil leaves and add to the yolk mixture. Melt the butter add the flour and cook for 1 minute. Remove from the heat and add the remainder of cream and the milk stir them over medium heat continuously until smooth and thick. Fill the egg whites with the yolk mixture and pour sauce over to serve. This dish can be served either hot or cold as a starter.

CASSEROLE OF CHICKEN WITH CHERVIL

25 g (1 oz) butter
15ml (1 tbsp) oil
1.4 kg (3 lb) chicken, jointed
2 Spanish onions
150 g (5 oz) carrots
30 ml (2 tbsp) chervil (fresh) or 15 ml (1 tbsp) dried
150 ml ($\frac{1}{4}$ pt) chicken stock
300 ml ($\frac{1}{2}$ pt) red wine

30 ml (2 tbsp) double cream
Sea salt and freshly ground black pepper
30 ml (2 tbsp) lemon juice

Heat the butter and oil in a heavy pan. Add the chicken pieces and cook until browned, then remove and keep warm. Slice the onions and carrots and add to pan turning until well coated with oil. Add the chervil, reserving a few small pieces for decoration. Heat the stock and wine together and pour into the pan. Return the chicken to the pan and simmer until tender – about 40 minutes.

Remove the chicken pieces and keep warm. Allow the liquid in the pan to cool slightly, then skim off the surface fat. Purée liquid and vegetables in a blender, then return to pan. Add the cream, season with salt and pepper and stir until heated through. Add the lemon juice and pour the sauce over the chicken pieces. Garnish with the chervil leaves that have been reserved. Serve with rice or new potatoes and a green vegetable or salad.

Poterium sanguisorba

SALAD BURNET

Family: Rosaceae

'The juice of the leaves doth cleanse and take away all spots
and freckles of the face and cause a good colour.'
– John Gerard

This herb is a native of the Mediterranean and southern Europe and was introduced to Britain in the sixteenth century. The Pilgrim Fathers took it with them to America where it now grows freely. Although it is mainly used as a salad herb, it was once commonly used medicinally and formed an important part of Tudor knot gardens.

Salad burnet is a short, greyish-green perennial which will reach a height of at most 40 cm (16 in). This and its other advantage of being an evergreen make it a useful addition to the garden. The coarsely-toothed leaflets are formed in a flat rosette, from the centre of which the new leaves and flowers spring. The flowers are petal-less, the upper part bearing red styles and the lower yellow stamens, and they bloom from May to September.

Cultivation

Salad burnet is best suited to a dry, light soil that has been well-limed, and it favours a position in full sunlight although it will tolerate shade. Sow from seed in the early spring and keep the soil well-watered. Once the seedlings can be handled, thin them out to about 30 cm (1 ft) apart.

For indoor cultivation, plant the seeds in a pot containing well-limed light soil or seed compost. Place in partial sunlight and do not allow the soil to become dry. When the seedlings are about 5 cm (2 in) high, nip out the growing points to encourage branching. Be warned, however, that the plant will not retain its compact shape for more than a few months, after which it will become straggly whatever you do, so have more seedlings ready to take its place.

Although salad burnet is a perennial, it is preferable to grow a new crop from seed each year because it is only the young leaves which are good for eating. On established plants, encourage leaf growth by removing the flower heads and the tough outer leaves, and remember that left to its own devices salad burnet will self-sow quite freely, particularly if several plants are growing together.

Uses

Salad burnet acts as a general tonic and blood purifier. After the gloomy winter months, snip a few leaves into a green salad for a natural lift rather than resorting to pills. During the summer, it can be used to ease the painful effect of sunburn; hold a compress soaked in a strong infusion of salad burnet to the burned skin and alternate every few minutes with a fresh cool pad until the pain subsides. The herb's gentle refining effect on the skin also makes it a good moisturizer.

SALAD BURNET MOISTURIZER

150 ml ($\frac{1}{4}$ pt) boiling water
45 ml (3 tbsp) fresh salad burnet leaves, chopped
1 egg yolk
5 ml (1 tsp) liquid honey
5 ml (1 tsp) almond oil

Make a strong infusion by pouring the boiling water over the salad burnet leaves and allow to stand for 15 minutes. Beat the egg yolk and mix with the honey. Add the almond oil. Strain the infusion and add the egg mixture. Use as you would a commercial moisturizer. It will last for several weeks if stored in a screw-top jar in the refrigerator.

Burnet Saxifrage

Small Burnet Saxifrage

The delicate flavour of salad burnet leaves, somewhere between a cucumber and an almond, makes it a useful herb in the kitchen. It should always be used fresh because it tastes bitter and unpleasant when cooked, and it goes best in salads or as a garnish to cheese and egg dishes or vegetable soups. It also makes a delightful addition to a fruit cup or summer punch bowl, and the coarsely chopped leaves are delicious served in a fruit salad. Apart from adding a particularly good flavour to cucumber, salad burnet leaves will reduce the indigestibility which some people find with cucumber sandwiches.

CUCUMBER SANDWICHES WITH SALAD BURNET

Cut very fine slices of wholemeal bread and butter them sparingly with unsalted butter. Peel the cucumber or wash well and thoroughly score the skin with a fork. Slice finely and fill sandwiches, seasoning with a few drops of lemon juice and finely-chopped fresh salad burnet leaves. As a variation, add a sprinkling of chives or sliced shallots.

CHEESE AND SALAD BURNET SAVOURY
(serves 4)

4 slices wholemeal bread
Butter for spreading
Cheddar cheese for topping
5 ml (1 tsp) salad burnet leaves
Tomato and cucumber slices

Toast one side of the bread. Butter the other side and cover with cheese. Melt under grill. Sprinkle with finely chopped salad burnet leaves and garnish with slices of cucumber and tomato.

PINEAPPLE DESSERT

Hollow out a whole pineapple and chop the flesh into cubes. Retain as much juice as possible. Add fresh fruits such as strawberries, orange segments, grapes or slices of apple and mix with caster sugar. Add chopped salad burnet leaves and the pineapple juice. Finally stir in 15 ml (1 tbsp) of kirsch or sweet white wine. Place mixture in pineapple shell to serve.

Poterium sanguisorba

Cichorium intybus

CHICORY

Family : Compositae

'These herbs when they are green have the virtue to cool
the hot burning of the liver.'
– John Gerard

This herb has been used for many centuries as a vegetable and in salads, and also as a pleasant-tasting coffee substitute. The ground roots added to coffee beans are believed to act as an antidote to the stimulant of caffeine, and chicory is widely used in France and other European countries for this purpose. The roots and leaves have a slightly bitter taste and the plant contains a milky sap which is indicative of the salad type of the Compositae family to which it belongs. With its high vitamin C and iron content, chicory is a valuable source of nutrition for both people and cattle.

Chicory grows throughout Europe and Asia, and has spread through North America. It is best treated as an annual, although wild chicory is a perennial, and will reach a height of 1–1.5 metres (3–5 ft). Its dark green, toothed leaves and bright blue flowers which appear from May to September are similar to those of the dandelion.

Cultivation
Chicory prefers a cool climate but will grow almost anywhere if the soil is well-prepared by deep digging. If humus is also added, the plants will grow more prolifically. Grow from seeds – which germinate easily and keep their germinating powers for several years – throughout the summer. Plant them in rows about 60 cm (2 ft) apart and about 1 cm ($\frac{1}{2}$ in) deep, and once about 10 leaves have appeared, heap up the soil around the plant in order to bleach the leaves and remove excess bitterness from the taste. Fortunately, chicory suffers little from garden pests and provided the surrounding soil is kept loose and free from weeds, there should be a plentiful supply of leaves for summer use.

For a winter supply of chicory, dig up the roots of some of the plants after the first frost has arrived. Cut off the tops to about 2.5 cm (1 in) of the crown and plant in a box of soil, kept in a dark place at a temperature of at least 10°C/50°F. The first new shoots will appear very quickly and these should be broken off to encourage new growth. The heart of tight white leaves should be used immediately it is cut off because once exposed to light the leaves will start to droop.

Uses
Chicory leaves make a nutritious and deliciously sharp-tasting salad and can be used on their own or added to other green salads. The hearts make a good and unusual vegetable: remove the cone-shaped wedge at the base of the heart before steaming or boiling in just enough water to cover for about 10 minutes. Add a few drops of lemon juice to the cooking water to enhance the flavour, and serve with butter or a cheese sauce.

CHICORY COFFEE
This has an attractive, distinctive aroma and will aid the digestion with none of the harmful effects of conventional coffee. Harvest the chicory roots in the autumn (*Cichorium intybus radicosum* has long thick roots and is particularly good to grow for this purpose) and leave them to dry. When they are brittle, grind them and roast them lightly. Use as you would ground coffee.

Cichorium intybus

MARJORAM

Family : Labiatae

'The Sweete Marjeromes are much used to please outward
senses in nosegayes, and in the windowes of houses.'
– John Parkinson

'The juyce thereof dropped into the eares easeth the paines
in them, and helpeth the singing noyse of them.'
– John Parkinson

The different types of marjoram have all developed from the parent plant, oregano or wild marjoram. A native of the Mediterranean region, it was used by the ancient Egyptians, Greeks and Romans not only as a food flavouring but as a healing herb with the power to cure many ailments, including the common cold and sore throats. It was introduced to Britain by the Romans and during the Middle Ages was grown for its perfume and beauty. Before the discovery of hops, marjoram was an essential ingredient in the brewing of beer, and dried ground marjoram has even been used as a substitute for snuff.

Today, marjoram grows wild in Mexico and parts of South America, where it spread from the North after being introduced there by the Pilgrim Fathers. It can also be seen growing wild in Algeria, Tunisia and parts of Egypt. The three main types of marjoram all have the same characteristic scent and flavour. Only sweet marjoram (*Origanum majorana*) is an annual, although in cooler climates the other two are best treated as annuals, and this is the smallest of the varieties. It will not grow much higher than 20 cm (8 in) and is a compact plant with small oval leaves and knot-like green flowers, and very strongly perfumed. Pot marjoram (*O. onites*) will reach 60 cm (2 ft) and has a tendency to sprawl. It bears a profusion of pink flowers and tiny whorls of leaves. Oregano (*O. vulgare*) is the tallest of the three and also has the strongest flavour. It will grow to a height of 75 cm (2½ ft) and in summer has deep purple flowers formed in clusters with darker bracts.

Cultivation

As marjoram comes from the Mediterranean it prefers a warm sheltered place to grow, preferably by a south-facing wall. Sweet marjoram requires a medium rich soil with a neutral balance. Propagate from seeds and give these an early start by planting them under glass in the early spring. Once the seedlings are established, plant them out and make sure that they are not allowed to dry out – constant humidity is important for their healthy development.

Pot marjoram, a perennial, will survive the winter in a temperate climate and prefers a dry light soil with some direct sunlight. It can be propagated from cuttings or from seeds – as with sweet marjoram, sow the seeds under glass in the early spring for the best start, particularly if your garden soil tends to be heavy. Alternatively, sow them directly into the soil, in drills about 1 cm (½ in) deep and 20 cm (8 in) apart. This is also a good plant to grow indoors. Use a light potting compost with some lime chippings added, water sparingly and place in a very sunny position. Keep it trimmed back to ensure a compact shape.

Oregano prefers to grow on poor chalky well-drained soil and like the other varieties needs an abundance of sunshine. Propagate it from cuttings taken in the autumn or early spring and keep them in the warm under glass until the roots are well formed. Although a slow plant to grow, its deliciously strong flavour, invaluable in many culinary dishes, makes it worth the trouble.

Harvest the marjoram leaves in the late summer when they contain the greatest concentration of goodness and collect the ripe seeds in the autumn ready for planting out the next year.

Uses

There are so many uses for marjoram that it is difficult

Origanum majorana

to select a few. A strong infusion of the herb will help ease the discomfort of earache, particularly if it is caused by the build-up of wax: make it by adding 10 ml (2 tsp) of dried leaves to one cup of boiling water, allow to stand for at least 10 minutes, then strain. Use warm two or three times a day until the condition is relieved.

MARJORAM OIL
A few drops of this fragrant oil applied directly to an aching tooth and the surrounding gums will help soothe the pain. (In an emergency, try chewing some fresh leaves to relieve the ache.)

400 ml ($\frac{2}{3}$ pt) almond oil or green olive oil
15 ml (1 tbsp) white wine vinegar
Large handful of fresh marjoram leaves

Put the oil in a 600 ml (1 pt) bottle. (A bottle with long sloping neck is preferable since it will prevent the herbs all rising to the top.) Bruise the marjoram leaves well with a pestle and mortar, and mix with the vinegar. Add the mixture to the oil and shake the bottle thoroughly. Stand the bottle in a sunny position for about a month, shaking it every day. Test that it is ready by rubbing some of the oil on the hand – if the fragrance lingers, it is 'fixed' and ready for use. Otherwise add some more crushed herb and leave for a further 2 weeks.

Marjoram leaves and flowers also make an effective moth bag. Fill small bags made of fine cotton with the dried marjoram, adding a few heads of lavender if you wish, and mix with 5 ml (1 tsp) of dried orris root to act as a 'stabiliser' so that the herbs do not release their essential oils too rapidly. For glossy

Bastard Marjoram

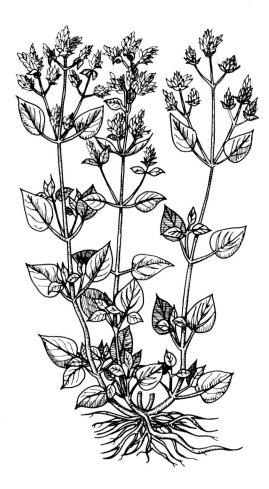

White Bastard Marjoram

hair, try massaging the scalp after shampooing with a strong infusion of marjoram (two handfuls of fresh leaves to one cup of boiling water). This treatment is particularly beneficial for those suffering from hair loss.

The spicy flavour of marjoram leaves and flowers is a boon to the cook. Since the herb also contains antiseptic properties, it has the added advantage of keeping away stomach upsets and generally purifying the bloodstream if included regularly in the diet. Fresh marjoram makes an attractive garnish and addition to salads, and the dried herb can be sprinkled over fish, poultry and game before grilling or roasting to give the food a delicious tang. It can be added to gravies, soups and casseroles, and will make a piquant addition to stuffings and sauces. Fresh, it enhances the flavour of hot cheese dishes and ome-

lettes, and can be added to vegetables during cooking. Perhaps, however, it is most famous for its affinity with tomatoes which is akin to that of basil. Remember that the strength of marjoram varies according to the type you use so go easy at first until you are familiar with it.

SPAGHETTI WITH MARJORAM (serves 4)

30 ml (2 tbsp) olive oil
1 clove garlic, crushed
1 large onion, finely chopped
450 g (1 lb) canned tomatoes
Salt and pepper
5 ml (1 tsp) fresh marjoram, or 2.5 ml ($\frac{1}{2}$ tsp) dried, chopped marjoram
350 g (12 oz) spaghetti
Parmesan cheese (optional)

English Wild Marjoram

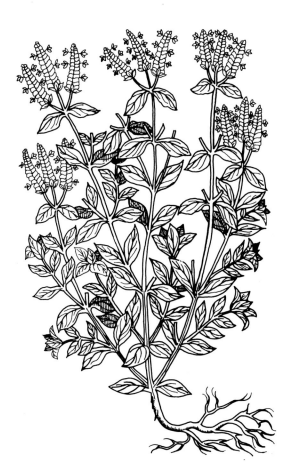

Wild Marjoram

Great Sweet Marjoram

Pot Marjoram

Heat the oil in a saucepan and add the garlic and onion; sauté until the onions are transparent. Stir in the tomatoes and their juice, pressing the tomatoes to break them up. Cook rapidly for 10 minutes when the liquid will begin to reduce. Season with salt and pepper, add the marjoram and keep warm. Boil the spaghetti in plenty of salted water until just tender. Drain and serve immediately with the sauce. Top with Parmesan cheese if liked.

BEEF CASSEROLE WITH MARJORAM AND BAY (serves 4)

4 rashers bacon
25 g (1 oz) butter
1 large onion, sliced
750 g (1½ lb) stewing beef
30 ml (2 tbsp) flour
150 ml (¼ pt) stock
125 g (4 oz) button mushrooms
2 sprigs marjoram, tied together
150 ml (¼ pt) red wine
1 bay leaf
Salt and pepper

Remove rind from bacon rashers and dice. Melt the

butter in a saucepan and fry the onion and bacon gently until brown. Cut the beef into small cubes. Remove onion and bacon from pan and brown beef, sprinkled with the flour. Transfer to a casserole and add all the other ingredients. Cover and cook in a moderate oven for at least 2 hours at 180°C/350°F (gas 4). Remove the marjoram and bay leaf before serving.

MARJORAM SCONES
Try adding marjoram to a basic scone mix for serving with casseroles and stews.

125 g (4 oz) self-raising flour
Pinch salt
50 g (2 oz) butter
Cold water
30 ml (2 tbsp) fresh marjoram leaves, chopped

Sift the flour and salt together. Rub in the butter until the mixture resembles fine breadcrumbs. Add sufficient cold water to make a dough and then add the marjoram. Stir quickly with a knife and roll out thickly. Cut into shapes and place on top of a casserole, cover and cook for ¾ hour.

Melissa officinalis

LEMON BALM

Family: Labiatae

'Baulme is often among other hot and sweete herbs, to make
baths and washings for mens bodies or legges, in the
Summertime, to warme and comfort the veines and sinewes.'
– John Parkinson

This highly fragrant herb came to Europe from the Middle East where it is still commonly used to make a refreshing tea. Its botanical name 'melissa' comes from the Greek word for bee and lemon balm was used in the ancient world and later by monks to attract bees and hence produce a particularly delicious honey. The Greeks would sometimes rub hives with the leaves of the plant to keep the bees happy and near home. Lemon balm was also used medicinally, to relieve headaches and tension and act as a general tonic, and it was one of the old strewing herbs to keep houses smelling sweet. The herb is associated with love and happiness and in the past lovers would wear armlets made from it.

Lemon balm is a medium-sized perennial herb. There are many types but most have yellowish-green oval pointed leaves with toothed edges, with flowers that vary from white to palest mauve. These grow from the base of each stem in leafy whorled spikes and bloom from July to September. At the end of the season the plant will reach about 60 cm (2 ft) in height.

Cultivation

Lemon balm is very easy to grow and if the roots are not contained may well begin to take over the garden. It will grow on any type of soil but will emit a stronger scent if grown on rich soil. Although it prefers a shady position, it will need a little sunshine to prevent it becoming blanched. Propagation can be from seed or by dividing a clump or taking a cutting. If growing from seed, sow in the early summer under the protection of a cold frame or cloche. The tiny seeds retain their germinating power for several years so fresh seeds are not necessary. They

are, however, slow to germinate and it will help to soak them overnight before planting in order to soften the hard outer casing. It may take up to 4 weeks before the seeds begin to sprout but once the seedlings are about 10 cm (4 in) high, they can be planted into

Balm

83

their permanent flowering position. In the first year there will be few leaves to pick but after that the plant will spread quickly and provide an abundant supply. Some leaves can be picked before the flowers open but the main crop should be harvested in the autumn when the plant should be cut right back. (In cold conditions, it will die back naturally.) The new shoots should be visible close to the soil and they should be protected from frost during the winter by covering with straw or compost. Once lemon balm is established in the garden, it is simplest to propagate by dividing a clump in the spring or autumn, or taking a stem cutting.

Although a strong-growing plant, lemon balm can be grown successfully indoors and in this case seeds can be grown all the year round. Use a moist lime-free soil and, once germinated, keep in a sunny position, trimming frequently so that the plant retains a compact shape. Do not repot into any pot larger than 10 cm (4 in) in diameter.

The leaves can be dried very successfully and will retain their delightful lemon scent for many months. Tie the older stems upside down in a dry airing cupboard and they will soon become crisp without losing their bright, yellow-green colour. When brittle, the leaves can be rubbed off the stems and stored in airtight jars in a dark cupboard.

Uses

Lemon balm's delightful fragrance makes it a pleasurable plant to have in the garden or the house, and a very useful herb to add to a pot-pourri or herb cushion. To promote a good night's sleep, make a cushion using a fine material such as muslin as an inner lining, which will enable the perfume to escape, and fill with a mixture of crushed lemon balm leaves, lemon thyme and rosemary leaves (removed from the stalks).

POT-POURRI WITH LEMON BALM

There is a limitless choice of herbs to accompany lemon balm but try a large handful of fragrant dried rose petals, such as those of the wild dog rose, and lavender flowers. Mix with the dried lemon balm leaves in an open bowl and add a fixative to prevent them from releasing their perfume and natural oils too quickly. Ground orris root, which is available from most herbalists, is good for this; add 15 ml

(1 tbsp) of it to every five cups (1.5 litres/2½ pints) of leaves and petals and for a spicy fragrance, add a little ground nutmeg or clove.

Medicinally, lemon balm leaves made into a tea will help soothe headaches and relieve tension, toothache and morning sickness in pregnancy. This is indeed a versatile herb, and in the Middle East lemon balm tea is traditionally believed to promote a long and happy life. Make it in the usual way, using 5 ml (1 tsp) of dried leaves or 15 ml (1 tbsp) of crushed fresh leaves to every cup of boiling water.

The subtle lemon flavour of balm means that it can be added generously to many dishes, sprinkled fresh on salads or laid across joints of meat such as lamb or pork for roasting.

Turkey Balm

POACHED WHITING IN BALM SAUCE
(serves 4)

2 sprigs parsley (fresh)
4 peppercorns
7.5 ml (1½ tsp) vinegar
1 sprig lemon thyme
1 bay leaf
5 ml (1 tsp) salt
600 ml (1 pt) water
4 fillets whiting
50 g (2 oz) butter
30 ml (2 tbsp) flour
1 large handful balm leaves, finely chopped

Place parsley, peppercorns, vinegar, thyme, bay leaf and salt into a pan with the water and bring to boil. Add the whiting and poach gently for 10 minutes until cooked through. Remove the fish and keep warm. Strain liquid and reserve. Melt butter in a small pan, stir in the flour and cook for 1 minute. Remove from heat and gradually whisk in reserved liquid. Return to heat and boil steadily for 5 minutes, stirring continuously. Remove from heat and add finely chopped balm leaves to sauce. Pour over whiting and serve.

LEMON BALM STUFFING
As a variation on the usual sage and onion stuffing or orange accompaniment to roast duck, try this old-fashioned recipe for a stuffing made with lemon balm leaves: it will counteract the fattiness of the duck and give it a delicate lemon flavour.

225 g (8 oz) uncooked prunes, stoned
225 g (8 oz) cooking apples, peeled and chopped
Large handful of lemon balm leaves, finely chopped
1 egg yolk

Mix together the prunes, apples and lemon balm leaves. Bind with egg yolk and allow to stand. Wash and dry the duck thoroughly, dust inside with flour and pack loosely with the mixture.

BALM WINE (makes 4.5 litres/1 gallon)
A delicious wine can be made from balm leaves picked in the early autumn.

Bastard Balm with purple flowers

2.2 litres (4 pts) balm leaves, crushed
1 lemon
1 orange
450 g (1 lb) raisins
1.4 kg (3 lb) sugar
4.5 litres (1 gallon) water
50 g (2 oz) yeast

Place the lemon balm leaves together with the rinds and juice of the lemon and orange, the raisins and the sugar in a preserving pan. Bring the water to the boil in a separate pan and add to the leaves and fruit. Stir and when cool (20°C/70°F), add the yeast. Cover and leave to ferment in a warm place (the airing cupboard is ideal) for 7 days. Siphon into a fermenting jar and plug the top of the jar with an air-lock (or cotton-wool if no air-lock is available). When the wine has cleared and there are no further bubbles, bottle, making sure to leave the deposit in the fermentation jar.

LIME

Family: Tiliaceae

'The leaves boiled in water with a piece of Alum and a little
honey cure the sores in childrens mouths.'
– John Gerard

Common lime, or linden, is a cultivated hybrid of two wild varieties, small-leaved and large-leaved lime, native to Britain. It now grows all over Europe and is sometimes found in Australia and North America. With a smooth, straight trunk and formally shaped branches, this beautiful tree may grow to as high as 50 metres (130 ft) if left unpruned. Although more common in parklands and ornamental woods where they are often planted in avenues, it is still possible to find lime trees growing wild by roadsides and in copses. In southern Europe they are often trained into hedges. Apart from being a decorative tree, lime contains many valuable ingredients and the leaves and flowers can be used in medicinal, cosmetic and culinary recipes.

Lime is a deciduous tree with soft, green, heart-shaped leaves and clusters of tiny drooping lemon-coloured flowers which appear from about June onwards, to be followed by the equally small velvety green fruit. The flowers have a strong fragrance, particularly attractive to bees, and hang downwards in clusters.

Cultivation

Lime prefers a moist loam soil and is generally propagated by layering. Do not prune the tree if it is being grown for its flowers and be prepared to wait for some time before it produces these.

Uses

Medicinally, lime flowers have many uses. Add a handful, firmly tied in a muslin bag, to the bathwater to act as a tonic. For a mild and natural aid to sleep and digestion, make a tisane with a handful of flowers added to 1 litre ($1\frac{3}{4}$ pt) of boiling water. This is a mild diuretic and is good for gout and rheumatism. It will also reduce cramp and relieve colds and headaches caused by tension.

LIME FACIAL TREATMENT

This will soften the skin and cleanse the pores. First ensure that the skin is thoroughly cleaned, using a non-greasy cleanser, pure soap or cleansing milk, and pat dry gently. Place 60 ml (4 tbsp) of lime flowers in a bowl and add 1 litre ($1\frac{3}{4}$ pt) of boiling water. Lean over the bowl and cover the head with a towel to trap in the steam. Remain in this position for at least 10 minutes to allow the steam to open and cleanse the pores, then wipe the skin with a cool damp cloth or, if preferred, dab it with skin freshener. Pat dry with a soft towel and allow the skin to cool down naturally for about 30 minutes before going outside.

In the kitchen the delicate aromatic flavour of lime leaves will give a lift to green salads, and a combination of lettuce leaves, chopped celery and chopped fresh lime leaves tossed in an oil and vinegar dressing makes a delicious accompaniment to cold meats and cheeses on a hot summer day. A few fresh lime leaves, washed and dried and with their stalks removed, make a tasty and nutritional sandwich filler; use them between slices of brown bread spread with unsalted butter and sprinkle with a little lemon juice.

For a refreshing and soothing tea, add 15 ml (1 tbsp) of fresh lime flowers or 5 ml (1 tsp) of dried to each cup of boiling water. Do not allow to steep for more than a few minutes or the delicate flavour will be lost.

Tilia cordata

SORREL

Family: Polygonaceae

'Sorrel doth undoubtedly cool and mightily dry, but because
it is sour it likewise cutteth the tough humours.'
– John Gerard

There are two main types of sorrel, French (*Rumex scutatus*) and garden or wild sorrel (*R. acetosa*). Of the two, French has the more pleasant flavour and is often used as a culinary herb. The ancient Egyptians, Greeks and Romans are known to have used it in cooking and medical recipes, and the plant contains vitamin C and other substances which make it valuable.

Sorrel is a small perennial herb, a member of the dock family and very similar in appearance to spinach with its shiny bright green, spade-shaped leaves and reddish stems. The tiny flowers appear from May onwards and last well into June, borne on long leafless spikes. Garden sorrel can be seen growing wild in pastures all over Europe and seeds itself vigorously, often becoming a pest to farmers.

Cultivation

Sorrel is an easy plant to grow, compact and neat in appearance, and an asset to the herb garden. Propagate it either from seeds planted in the spring or from root division in the autumn. The seeds take only about 2 weeks to germinate and within a month the seedlings should be strong enough to be transplanted to a sunny corner of the garden. At this stage water them well and protect them from slugs and other garden pests, which find the juicy leaves irresistible.

Uses

Sorrel is a mild antiseptic, blood cleanser and kidney stimulant. A warm poultice of sorrel leaves will draw abscesses, boils and similar skin eruptions quickly to a head: chop a handful of fresh leaves, moisten with boiling water and apply to the affected area. An infusion taken internally is a good remedy for acne, eczema and minor skin disorders. Add 25 g (1 oz) fresh chopped sorrel leaves to 1.1 litres (2 pt) boiling water and allow to infuse for 10 minutes; strain and sip a cupful three times a day

Sorrel is also useful as a polish and stain remover. To clean wicker or bamboo furniture, and to shine silver, boil some sorrel leaves in water and use a cloth soaked in the solution; leave to dry and polish off with

French Sorrel

Rumex scutatus

Garden Sorrel

Knobbed Sorrel

a clean dry cloth. To remove ink stans from clothes, rub the material with sorrel leaves and then with household soap, rinse off and repeat as necessary.

The slightly sour, tangy flavour of sorrel is particularly appreciated by French cooks and the herb is often sold in French markets. It is used to make a delicious sauce to accompany fish, poultry and white meat, but it is best-known as the basis of a thick and nutritious soup.

SORREL SOUP (serves 6)

75 g (3 oz) butter
450 g (1 lb) fresh sorrel leaves, coarsely chopped
1 large onion, finely chopped
25 g (1 oz) flour
1 sprig of rosemary
2.2 litres (4 pt) water
1 egg, beaten
15 ml (1 tbsp) sour cream or natural yoghurt

Melt the butter in a large pan and add the sorrel leaves, onion, flour and rosemary. Sauté for 5 minutes. Boil the water and add to the pan. Simmer gently for half an hour and then remove the rosemary. Take off the heat and allow to cool slightly. Before serving, mix the egg and cream or yoghurt and stir into the soup over a gentle heat. Do not boil.

Sheeps Sorrel

Archangelica officinalis

ANGELICA

Family: Umbelliferae

'The roote of garden Angelica is a singular remedie against
poison, and against the plague, and all infections taken by evil
and corrupt aire, if you do but take a peece of the roote and
holde it in your mouth, or chew the same between your teeth,
it doth most certainly drive away the pestilentiall aire.'
– John Gerard

Angelica is one of the oldest and largest of our herbs. It originated in the cold countries of northern Europe where it is a well-known antidote to rheumatism and the associated ills of the raw, damp climates of the northern hemisphere. It was brought to England in the sixteenth century and now also grows profusely in the Alps and Pyrenees. In the past the roots and seeds of angelica were burned in the home to fill it with sweet perfume and during the plague the roots were chewed as a preventative medicine and even as an attempted cure. Today it is cultivated mostly for its leaves and stalks which are crystallised and used as cake decorations.

An imposing, handsome biennial, angelica can reach 2.5 metres (8 ft) in height. Its thick green stems are sometimes tinged with purple and it has bright green, broadly toothed leaves, whose leaflets spring from the stalks in impressive sheaths. The pale green flowers appear in July and last until September, arranged in flattened clumps of florets, and will usually come in the second year although since angelica is encouraged as a perennial even though strictly a biennial, they may not appear until the third or fourth year.

Cultivation

The easiest method of propagation is by root division of a mature plant, since angelica seeds quickly lose their germinating power. However, this can be overcome by planting the seeds within a few days of their ripening or by storing them in an airtight bag in a cool place until they are wanted. If using stored seeds, sow in the early spring but fresh seeds can be planted either then or in the autumn, although with autumn planting they will grow more slowly. Plant them about 2.5 cm (1 in) deep in rich, moist soil, ideally where there is a combination of shade and sun, and not too close together. They will take time in germinating so do not be impatient. Keep them moist at all times and once the seedlings have developed, lift them carefully and space them out. Remember that they are large plants and better situated at the back of the border.

Pinch out the centre of young plants to encourage a bushy growth, and once angelica begins to produce flowers, it is best to pick off the buds to prevent the plant seeding and to encourage it as a perennial. If allowed to seed, the plant will die off.

Uses

Dried angelica leaves make a fragrant addition to a pot-pourri and their scent blends particularly well with that of dried rose petals to sweeten our homes, just as it sweetened homes in the past. Firmly secured in a muslin bag, they can also be used to scent the bathwater.

Medicinally, angelica is also useful. Fresh crushed leaves can be applied as a compress to relieve asthma and chest congestion, and angelica tea is beneficial for many ailments, from rheumatism, colds and chest infections, flatulence and indigestion, to nervous tension. Make it by adding a cup of boiling water to 5 ml (1 tsp) of dried leaves; allow to stand for 5–10 minutes.

In the kitchen, angelica is best known as a sweetmeat but it can also be used as a vegetable. The freshly picked young leaves are delicious when simmered gently in a little lightly salted water until tender, and the young stalks can be braised like celery and served

Garden Angelica

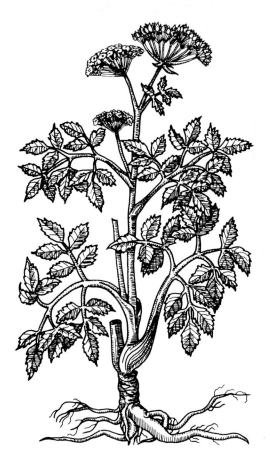

Wild Angelica

with a white sauce as an accompaniment to a grill or roast dish.

CRYSTALLISED ANGELICA

It is easy, if time-consuming, to make your own crystallised angelica to decorate cakes and sweets, rather than buying commercial products. Always use young green stems from a plant in its second year of growth.

Young angelica stems
Sugar
Caster sugar, for sprinkling
Water

Cut the stems into pieces up to 15 cm (6 in) long and soak overnight in cold water. Drain and plunge into a pan of boiling water; simmer until tender. Drain and when cool, peel off the outer skin. (If the skin will not come away easily, repeat the process.)

Make a syrup by boiling 225 g (8 oz) sugar with 300 ml ($\frac{1}{2}$ pt) water for 5–7 minutes. Place the peeled angelica stems in the syrup and leave for 24 hours. Drain, retaining the liquid. Heat the syrup to 102°C/

220°F and pour over the angelica pieces. Allow to cool, then drain. Repeat this whole process three times but on the third time, heat the syrup to 118°C/245°F, add the angelica pieces to the pan and boil for 10 minutes until stalks are translucent. Remove from the heat and allow to cool. Drain and when the angelica is almost dry, place on greaseproof paper, dust with caster sugar and put in a very cool oven 110°C/225°F (gas $\frac{1}{4}$) until thoroughly dried. Allow to cool completely before storing.

ANGELICA LIQUEUR

450 g (1 lb) fresh angelica stalks
600 ml (1 pt) brandy
350 g (12 oz) sugar

Cut the young stalks into fine pieces and add to the brandy in a hermetically sealed bottle. Leave in a sunny spot for about 2 weeks. Dissolve the sugar in a little water and add to the bottle. Leave to stand for a further 4 weeks, then filter and keep the liqueur in an airtight bottle.

Archangelica officinalis

Artemisia abrotanum

SOUTHERNWOOD

Family: Compositae

'This herb, burnt to ashes and mixed with oil, will promote the
growth of hair in person affected by baldness.'
– Bancakes Herbal

Southernwood is a native of southern France and the Mediterranean regions, where it can still be found growing wild. It was often used by herbalists in the past for its antiseptic and pesticidal properties, as well as by cooks who appreciated its rather bitter flavouring. In particular it was associated with remedies for gynaecological ailments, and was also believed to protect the home from witches and evil spirits – the herb would be strewn liberally on floors and hung above the threshold as a safeguard. Today it is grown more as an ornamental garden plant and is familiarly called Old Man or Lad's Love.

When mature, this perennial shrub will reach about 90 cm (3 ft) in height, with woody stems and fine, dusty green, feathery leaves. During the summer months it emits a strong bitter lemon scent from its leaves but unfortunately in temperate climates the tiny yellow florets rarely bloom.

Cultivation

Southernwood is very easy to grow and will not flag even in the dirt and grime of a city atmosphere. Propagate it from cuttings in the late spring or early autumn. Select the youngest woody stems, about 25 cm (10 in) long, making sure to include a heel; dip them in a hormone rooting powder and pot in light sandy compost. Southernwood benefits from full sunlight so try to situate it in a south-facing corner of the garden. Once established it will survive even in the stoniest and driest soil, but if kept moist, it will reward you with a luxurious crop of tender green fronds throughout the summer. At the end of the season, in late autumn, cut out the old wood to promote fresh young growth the following year.

Southernwood also makes an attractive foliage plant for container or indoor growing. Plant several cuttings in the same spot and trim the plants before they grow too tall; if at this early stage they are not allowed to exceed about 15 cm (6 in), they will become thick and bushy. Keep the soil damp and place the pot in a sunny position.

Uses

Southernwood and its milder sister, wormwood, are both powerful insect repellents. If you keep chickens, try planting a few bushes near the poultry enclosure to protect them from fleas. The dried leaves can be used to make moth bags; stored amongst clothing, the strong smell of ether they emit will repel moths.

Medicinally, southernwood is an antiseptic and stimulant. A tea made with the herb will act as a general tonic and help those recovering from 'flu to regain their strength and ease the aching limbs that accompany the condition. It is also said to eradicate worms, and relieve menstrual cramps and tension. Make the tea with 15 ml (1 tbsp) of dried leaves (and flowers if available) to each cup of boiling water. The taste is rather bitter so sweeten it with a little honey, but it is well worth drinking for the benefits it brings.

One of the powers which southernwood is reputed to possess is the ability to cure baldness. It is a common ingredient in today's hair lotions and, although it may not restore your hair, an infusion of southernwood certainly makes an excellent hair rinse, particularly for blondes.

The strongly aromatic leaves of southernwood are sometimes used in cooking but their bitter flavour is rather an acquired taste, so if you are unsure about it, try adding a couple of leaves with other herbs in a green salad before experimenting further.

Wild Southernwood

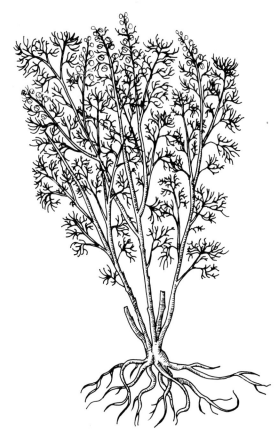

Male Southernwood

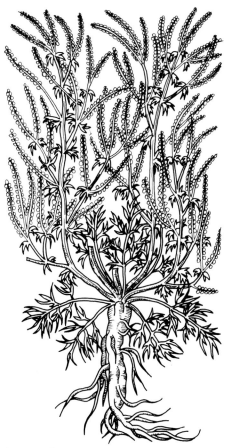

Female Southernwood

Unsavoury Southernwood

LEMON GERANIUM

Family: Geraniaceae

In the past, ladies and gentlemen would often carry bunches of sweet-scented geraniums in order to protect themselves from the evil smells and germs of dirty streets and open sewers. Recent tests have confirmed the wisdom of our predecessors for they show that in the perfume exhaled by such geranium posies are molecules of its essential oils that contain antiseptic properties.

There are two types of lemon-scented geranium: *Pelargonium limonium*, which is a large bush that can reach 1.5–1.75 metres (5–6 ft) and has large, deeply serrated leaves, and *P. crispum variegata*, which is a compact, creeping plant with small, variegated leaves. Both are hardy perennials and are covered with tiny lilac flowers in the spring.

Cultivation

Lemon-scented geraniums will readily withstand heat and drought, but they should be protected from frosts, so place them by a south-facing wall or bring them indoors before the winter frosts can kill them. Propagate by taking stem cuttings throughout the latter part of the year from September onwards. Sever young cuttings cleanly with a sharp knife, ensuring that a good heel of old wood is attached, and dip them in a hormone rooting powder before planting in a light sandy potting medium to encourage rapid root development. They can also be be rooted successfully by layering: find a downward bending stem and peg it to the soil, water well at the point where the stem meets the ground and as soon as the new roots have developed and the young plant has formed, it can be severed from the parent plant. This is a herb that because of its strong perfume is not bothered by insects so it can be planted prominently in the herb garden.

Uses

Lemon-scented geraniums are a natural antiseptic: bruise the leaves and apply them as a poultice to cuts and grazes. They will also make a refreshing and relaxing bath. Cut a piece of cheesecloth or muslin 20 cm (8 in) square, fill it with a handful of crushed leaves and, bringing the corners of the cloth together, secure firmly with a rubber band or ribbon. Either place the bag in a hot bath, letting the heat draw the perfume from the herb, or simply fill up the bath as usual and scrub yourself with the bag. When the herbs have released their goodness they can be discarded and the bag reused.

The leaves are useful in flower arranging and look particularly beautiful when added to bright spring flowers – irises, daffodils, etc.

In the kitchen lemon-scented geranium leaves have many decorative uses. Use small, perfect leaves to garnish desserts, such as sorbets and ices, or float them on fruit cups and punches. Add a leaf to milk puddings and egg custards to enhance the flavour, and for special dinners, arrange individual pats of butter on the leaves for an attractive table-setting.

Pelargonium limonium

Calendula officinalis

MARIGOLD

Family: Compositae

'The floures and leaves of Marigolds being distilled, the water
dropt into red and watery eyes, ceaseth the inflammation
and taketh away the pain.'
– Gerard

This popular plant, with its brilliantly coloured flowers, originally came from India where it was used by those of the Hindu faith to decorate their temples and holy places. The Romans used it as an inexpensive food colourant, a substitute for saffron, and it was they who introduced it to other parts of Europe. During the Middle Ages it continued to be used as a food colourant, particularly for soups and sauces, and it was also applied to old wounds and scars, for marigold contains healing properties as well as having culinary and cosmetic value.

Marigold is an annual herb which today grows wild in temperate climates. There are several varieties but on average they grow to a height of about 50 cm (20 in), with fleshy leaves and colourful daisy flowers which range from lemon yellow to deep orange, borne on a single upright stalk. The flowers, which open only during the day, appear in June and will last well into the autumn if the dead flower heads are picked off.

Cultivation

One of the easiest of all herbs to grow, marigold prefers a loamy soil and a position in full sunlight, although it will survive on heavy clay and in the shade. It seeds itself freely and will come up each year of its own accord, but the flowers of these later plants will tend to revert back to single heads. Propagate by seed sown in the spring and thin the seedlings out to about 45 cm (18 in) apart.

A tidy, compact plant with a continual supply of attractive flowers throughout the summer, marigold makes an excellent container-grown plant for pots or window-boxes. Remember to snap off the withered flowers to encourage further blooms and a bushy growth.

The flowers – which are the most useful part of the plant – can be harvested as they open fully and dried rapidly in a warm dark airy place; if exposed to sunlight their colour will not be preserved.

Uses

Marigold has a wealth of therapeutic uses. The flowers contain antiseptic properties and the seeds encourage blood clotting, which has caused it to be used for centuries to speed up the healing of wounds. In 1886 in the American West a Dr Reynolds reported in his medical journal on the use of marigold compresses to stop the bleeding of bullet wounds, and an ointment of marigold had long been known to help heal ulcers, cuts and cold sores.

MARIGOLD TEA

Apart from being a soothing drink, this can be applied cold to cuts and bruises, and the same mixture will also ease tired and swollen feet and painful chilblains, and reduce the inflammation of spots. But taken as a tea, with a little honey added if liked, it is beneficial to the heart and will ease menstrual pains and generally improve the complexion. Make it by pouring 600 ml (1 pt) of boiling water over 5–10 ml (1–2 tsp) of chopped marigold petals, and allow to infuse thoroughly before using.

The oil in marigold petals is especially beneficial to sensitive skins and there are many cosmetic recipes using this herb. Some crushed marigold petals added to an unperfumed cold cream will cleanse and soften the skin, as well as having a soothing effect on sunburn and minor burns. If the hands are rinsed in a

Calendula officinalis

Greater Double Marigold

Double Globe Marigold

marigold infusion, made like the tea, after washing up every day, rough and chapped skin can be avoided.

For a relaxing home massage, fill a 300 ml ($\frac{1}{2}$ pt) jar with marigold flowers and top up with sweet almond oil; place on a sunny windowsill for about 3 weeks, shaking every other day, then pour into a pan and heat until the flowers are crisp. Strain and bottle.

MARIGOLD FACE PACK

15 ml (1 tbsp) fresh marigold petals
1 egg
15 ml (1 tbsp) oatmeal
5 ml (1 tsp) wheatgerm oil

Crush the marigold petals and pour a little boiling water over them; allow to infuse for 10 minutes. Add the beaten egg, oatmeal and wheatgerm oil, and mix thoroughly. Apply to the face and neck after thoroughly washing the skin and allow to dry for 15 minutes before rinsing off with tepid water. Pat dry with a soft towel. The skin will feel soft and thoroughly cleansed.

In the kitchen, marigold petals continue to be a useful substitute for saffron to give colour to rice and other dishes. The edible flower will also add an attractive splash of colour to green salads.

Single Marigold

Mentha

MINT

Family: Labiatae

'It is good against watering eyes, and all manor of breakings
out in the head and against the infirmities of the fundament,
it is a sure remedie for childrens sore heads.'
– John Gerard

The many varieties of this popular fragrant herb all originate from one parent stock, a native of the Far East, which found its way via North Africa to Europe where it is now one of the most familiar of our herbs. It is named after the nymph, Minthe, who according to the legend was transformed into the plant, and it was used in the past as it still is today as a digestive aid. To the English, mint is traditionally associated with roast lamb, but the herb also has healing properties which have made it an ingredient in many old medical recipes.

The main types of mint are apple mint (*Mentha rotundifolia*), spearmint (*M. spicata*) and peppermint (*M. piperita*). Apple mint is a lovely, soft-textured plant with light green, downy leaves which, unlike the other varieties, are round and may be prettily variegated with cream. The ridged stem of the plant is downy and dark red, and at midsummer this mint will be covered with spikes of lilac flowers. It has a delicious strong scent and tastes of ripe apples. Peppermint and spearmint are also attractive plants. The former grows to about 60 cm (2 ft), with a smooth red stem, dark green leaves and pinky mauve flowers whose fresh smell greatly attracts bees. Both this and the better-known spearmint have long been grown for their essential oils. The latter is slightly smaller – growing to about 45 cm (18 in) – with bright green smooth leaves and spikes of lilac flowers.

Cultivation

All mints enjoy a light, rich soil that has been well dug and is partially shaded. They take a lot of nutrients out of the soil so prepare it thoroughly before planting by digging in compost and replenishing it with fertilizer from time to time to keep the plants

healthy. Propagate from an existing plant either by pulling up pieces of the long suckers, which will readily root themselves in the ground, or by severing parts of the roots using a sharp spade. Lay these runners in drills 8 cm (3 in) deep and water thoroughly

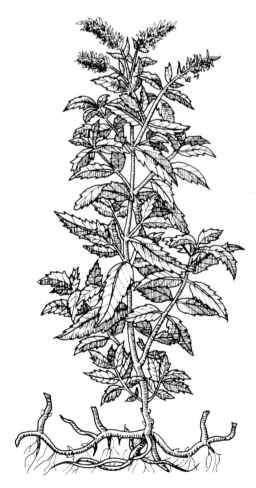

Spearmint

until the tiny new shoots appear. Mint soon gets out of control so restrict it by pushing tiles vertically into the soil around the plant or contain it by using a bottomless bucket or clay pot sunk in the ground.

Harvest sparingly during the first year of growth to allow the plant to establish itself, and pick the leaves before the flowers appear when they are at their peak. (Avoid picking them after rain as they are likely to turn black and go mouldy.) Mint, apart from apple mint, is liable to rust disease, so keep a look out for it, and should it occur, dig up and burn the whole plant. Its presence will be obvious from the increasing discoloration of the stems and leaves, and the roots will be soft and rotten when dug up

The plant will die down in the winter but to maintain a supply of mint through the winter, plant a few runners in a pot containing a rich potting compost and keep it indoors. Cut off the suckers as they appear in order to keep the plant bushy and pinch it down to 25 cm (10 in). Make sure it is well watered, and if aphids are attracted to it, wash them off with a mild solution of soap and water. Apple mint, with its small compact shape and delicate perfume, grows particularly well indoors, and another very attractive variety for indoor growing is the ornamental Corsican Mint (*Mentha requienii*). This tiny, moss-like plant has a lovely sharp flavour and will cover the pot with a blanket of bright leaves.

Uses

There are many medicinal and cosmetic uses for mint apart from its value in the kitchen. Peppermint makes an excellent addition to a pot-pourri or herb pillow: mix it with a little thyme, woodruff and lemon verbena or lavender, to which 5 ml (1 tsp) of orris should be added as a fixative, for a long-lasting and delightful fragrance. Try chewing a few leaves of spearmint, which contain the essential oil menthol used in mouthwashes and toothpastes, for sweet breath. To relieve tired, sore feet, make an infusion of 2 litres ($3\frac{1}{2}$ pts) of boiling water to 15 ml (1 tbsp) of fresh mint, allow to stand for 15 minutes, and then soak the feet in the warm fragrant infusion for 20 minutes. A stronger infusion 400 ml ($\frac{2}{3}$ pt) boiling water to 45–60 ml (3–4 tbsp) of fresh mint or 15 ml (1 tbsp) of dried makes an effective astringent lotion, good for removing ingrained dirt or counteracting an over-greasy skin. If your skin is sensitive, use a weaker solution.

The benefits of mint tea have been known for centuries. It will stimulate the gastric juices and thereby lessen flatulence and help digestion. Make it as you would ordinary tea – unless you have a very sweet tooth it will not need sweetening – and sip it hot after meals instead of coffee, or drink it iced with your meal.

Mint is indispensable in the kitchen. Its strong fresh flavour is very distinctive and it is rarely mixed with other herbs. A sprig of mint added to boiled, especially new, potatoes, to spring carrots and of course to peas will make them taste delicious. For a winter supply of the English speciality, mint sauce, to accompany roast lamb and lamb chops, make several pots of it in the summer when the mint is at its best and seal in hot sterilized jars to preserve.

Red Garden Mint

Illustration by Zane Carey

Mentha spicata

MINT SAUCE

30 ml (2 tbsp) fresh mint leaves, finely chopped
5 ml (1 tsp) caster sugar
15 ml (1 tbsp) wine vinegar

Stir the caster sugar into the vinegar until completely dissolved and add the chopped mint leaves. Sweeten more if necessary and store in airtight jars.

FIZZY MINT CUP (4 large glasses)

30 ml (2 tbsp) chopped fresh mint
5 ml (1 tsp) sugar
150 ml ($\frac{1}{4}$ pt) boiling water
Juice of 1 large orange or 2 small
Juice of 1 lemon
850 ml ($1\frac{1}{2}$ pt) ginger ale or soda water
6 ice cubes
4 sprigs mint

Mix the mint with the sugar in a large jug and pour over the boiling water. Allow to cool then add the fruit juices. Chill for 2 hours in the refrigerator, then strain and add the ginger ale or soda water and ice cubes. Pour into glasses and decorate each one with a sprig of fresh mint.

GREEN PEA SOUP WITH MINT (serves 4)

225 g (8 oz) fresh or frozen peas
850 ml ($1\frac{1}{2}$ pt) chicken stock
3 sprigs of mint
1 egg yolk
150 g (5 oz) natural yoghurt
5 ml (1 tsp) sugar
Sea salt and pepper

Cook the fresh peas for 10 minutes frozen peas for 5 minutes in a little lightly salted boiling water. (If you prefer to use dried peas, use 150 g/5 oz and soak first overnight.) Purée for a minute in an electric blender. Return to the pan and add the chicken stock. Chop the mint very finely, add to the soup and bring to the boil. Add sugar and simmer for a few minutes. Stir the egg yolk into the yoghurt and add a little of the hot soup. Mix, then pour back into the soup, stirring. Bring just to boil. Season and serve.

Small Horse Mint

LEMON AND MINT SORBET (serves 4–6)

300 ml ($\frac{1}{2}$ pt) water
3 strips lemon rind
75 g (3 oz) sugar
60 ml (4 tbsp) honey
5 ml (1 tsp) gelatine
300 ml ($\frac{1}{2}$ pt) fresh mint leaves
150 ml ($\frac{1}{4}$ pt) lemon juice
1 egg white

Bring half the water and the lemon rind to boil in a small pan. Stir in sugar until thoroughly dissolved and continue to boil for 5 minutes. Soak gelatine in 15 ml (1 tbsp) cold water. Combine with honey and add to lemon syrup in pan. Stir until dissolved. Wash the mint leaves and blend in an electric blender with the rest of the water. Strain the liquid into the lemon syrup, add the lemon juice and allow the mixture to cool. Remove rind, then freeze until almost frozen. Remove from freezer and mash with a fork. Fold in one stiffly beaten egg white until thoroughly incorporated then return to freezer and finish freezing. Allow to thaw a little before serving.

Anthemis nobilis ; Matricaria chamomilla

CHAMOMILE

Family : Compositae

'Oil of Camomile is exceeding good against all maner of ache
and paine, bruisings, shrinking of sinews, hardnesse and
colde swellings.'
– John Gerard

This fragrant, creeping herb – the name comes from the Greek 'chamai' meaning 'on the ground' – can be found growing wild all over Europe. There are two different types, of which true chamomile (*Matricaria chamomilla*) has valuable medicinal properties. It is said to be under the sign of the Sun and was esteemed by the ancient Egyptians, who dedicated it to the gods. It was also one of the Saxon sacred herbs, and was used for many centuries as a strewing herb, its sweet scent and antiseptic powers helping to freshen homes when ventilation and hygiene were inadequate. Roman chamomile (*Anthemis nobilis*) lacks the medicinal value of true chamomile but makes a delightful lawn. Its evergreen brightness will last throughout the year, it seldom needs mowing and it thrives from being walked over, when it will release its distinctive clove-like fragrance. One of the most famous chamomile lawns is at Buckingham Palace.

Roman chamomile is a perennial, true chamomile an annual, but they look very similar. Both have feathery leaves and yellow and white flowers, rather like miniature chrysanthemums, which last from about May until September. They are distinguished by the flowering heads, which in true chamomile are formed of single ray-florets and in Roman chamomile of double white florets.

Cultivation

Chamomile is extremely easy to grow provided the soil is not too wet and the temperature not too cold. To plant a lawn of Roman chamomile, the ground should be well-raked and weeded – once the lawn is established, it will be difficult to rid it of weeds. Sow in the early spring; the seeds germinate easily and the lawn should be quickly established. If only a small patch of lawn is wanted, it is also possible to separate the roots of an existing plant and transplant it to the desired position. This will soon spread to form a carpet of fragrant, evergreen leaves.

True chamomile can be cultivated similarly, and once a plant has flowered it will self-seed for the next year's growth. It is known that chamomile helps encourage the growth of nearby seedlings and improves the condition of neighbouring plants, so you may prefer not to keep it in a separate part of the garden.

Chamomile also grows well indoors and will thrive under fluorescent lights. The stems and young leaves form a pretty rosette and, with its feathery leaves and attractive flowers, the plant will cheer up the kitchen windowsill. Plant a few seeds in a pot or propagation box and they should germinate within a week. Once four leaves have developed, transplant the seedling to a larger pot filled with a light sandy soil mix. Keep the soil moist but do not allow the plants to stand in water. Cuttings can be removed from the maturing plant and will root rapidly, so that you will not have to bother with growing again from seed.

Uses

True chamomile is a useful herb for calming gastrointestinal disorders and acting as a general soother and aid to sleep. The mild and beneficial powers of chamomile tea were well known to Beatrix Potter, whose Peter Rabbit was sent off to bed by his mother with a dose of this tea after he had eaten too many of Mr McGregor's beans and radishes! Make the tea by pouring a cup of boiling water over 5 ml (1 tsp) of chamomile flowers, either fresh or dried; allow to

Chamomile

Roman Chamomile

steep for up to 5 minutes, then strain and drink while hot. A strong infusion made from chamomile and boiling water (see Hand Cream recipe below) will also ease the discomfort of earache; use a few warmed drops of the infusion several times a day until relief is given. Used cool, the infusion will reduce inflammation of the eyes; soak pads of lint in it and hold over the eyelids for a few minutes.

Chamomile also has skin-care uses. Some of the freshly picked flowers, tied in a muslin or cheese-cloth bag and hung beneath the hot water tap, will scent the bathwater and soothe and cleanse the skin. A little yarrow can be added to the bag to act as an astringent for those with greasy skins.

CHAMOMILE HAND CREAM
This cream will soften and whiten the hands, apart from smelling sweet. Make a strong infusion of chamomile by adding one cup of boiling water to 15 ml (1 tbsp) of freshly picked flowers. Allow to cool, then strain. Heat 30 ml (2 tbsp) lemon juice, 15 ml (1 tbsp) cocoa butter and 15 ml (1 tbsp) almond oil;

add the infusion, remove from the heat and stir continuously until the cream is smooth. When cool, store in a screw-topped jar.

CHAMOMILE SHAMPOO
Both this shampoo and the conditioning rinse given below will bring lustre to lifeless, out of condition hair. Make the shampoo by mixing 15 ml (1 tbsp) of pure soap flakes, 25 g (1 oz) of crushed chamomile flowers and 15 ml (1 tbsp) of borax. Add 300 ml ($\frac{1}{2}$ pt) of boiling water and stir until a froth has formed. Use as you would a usual shampoo, making sure that on the final rinse all the soap is removed. Add a squeeze of lemon juice to the last cool-water rinse for an extra shine.

CHAMOMILE CONDITIONING RINSE
Boil 25 g (1 oz) of chamomile flowers, dried or fresh, in 850 ml (1$\frac{1}{2}$ pt) water for 15 minutes. Allow to cool, strain and use as a final rinse for freshly shampooed hair. The lovely chamomile scent will linger in the hair.

Matricaria chamomilla

Petroselinum crispum

PARSLEY

Family: Umbelliferae

'The leaves are pleasant in sauces and broth, they are also
delightful to the taste and agreeable to the stomach.'
– John Gerard

Parsley is probably the most widely used of all the herbs. Not only is it attractive with its thick, bright-green, curly leaves – which makes it a good edging plant – but also it contains large quantities of vitamins A, B and C, iron and other essential minerals. Parsley was valued as a tonic in ancient Rome and for centuries it has been used to cure a great variety of human ailments. Legend has it that a little parsley eaten every day increases the virility of males and the fertility of females. It is in constant demand by cooks throughout the world as a flavouring and garnish because its subtle taste enhances even the blandest dish without overpowering it.

A native of the Mediterranean, parsley now grows throughout large parts of Europe and North America. It is a hardy biennial (although it is usually treated as an annual) and like all umbellifers it has a long tap root. In some varieties of parsley, the root is also used for eating.

Cultivation
Parsley has a reputation for being difficult to grow but with rich, well-drained soil and a little patience the seeds will germinate successfully, if at first slowly. To speed up germination, the seeds can be soaked overnight before planting or placed between sheets of wet blotting paper and kept in the refrigerator for a few days beforehand. However, the most important factor is the soil, which must be moist, rich in humus and well-dug so that the roots can penetrate easily. Plant the seeds in the spring when the last frosts are over, preferably in a sunny position, and in drills 1 cm ($\frac{1}{2}$ in) deep. For the first couple of weeks water them with hot water to help the germination process. Once the seedlings have begun to thicken, they can

be thinned out, but handle them with care. Mature plants will not transplant willingly because of the long tap root and they will also probably need to be covered with cloches in winter to protect them from frost. The plants will run to seed by the end of their second year, so to maintain a good supply, plant new seeds each year.

Parsley can also be grown indoors, in which case it will require a pot that is at least 10 cm (4 in) deep, soil that is acidic and feeding with a high nitrate fertilizer. While the seeds are germinating, the pot should be placed in a sunny position but once they have started to grow and thicken, it can be moved into partial shade. Reseed every few months to keep up the supply.

Uses
With its high vitamin and iron content, parsley has long been a valuable general tonic. It will stimulate the digestion and help the kidneys to function, and a little parsley added to the bath is reputed to relieve rheumatism. A cup of parsley tea sipped regularly will help ease the discomfort of haemorrhoids, and a cold infusion of freshly picked and crushed parsley leaves strained and used as an eyebath will help clear bloodshot eyes. The crushed leaves can also be applied directly to a sprain and the juice squeezed on to insect bites to bring quick relief. For those with oily skins, a strong infusion of parsley mixed with an equal amount of egg white and applied to the face and neck will act as a face pack. Leave it on for 15 minutes before rinsing off thoroughly with warm water and it will cleanse the skin and tighten up open pores. It has even been claimed that the face pack will remove freckles.

Mountain Parsley

Wild Parsley

Garden Parsley

Garden Parsley

HAIR CONDITIONER

Make an infusion of parsley by pouring 300 ml ($\frac{1}{2}$ pt) boiling water on to 60 ml (4 tbsp) chopped parsley leaves; allow to steep in an earthenware or china bowl for about 30 minutes, then strain. This will store in the refrigerator for up to a week in a screw-topped bottle. Use the infusion as a final rinse after shampooing and it will leave the hair glossy and will help to combat dandruff.

In the kitchen parsley is an indispensable herb and has the added advantage that it can be frozen – preferable to drying – although once defrosted it should be used immediately. It can be added generously to many savoury dishes and will counteract fattiness in foods or soften the flavour of strong tastes like garlic and onion. It can be chopped and sprinkled on to soups and stews as a garnish and whole sprigs used to decorate fish, meat and egg dishes, or encircle plates of sandwiches and savoury snacks – in some cases the garnishes may well contain more vitamins than the food itself.

For those cooks who want a hot garnish for their hot dishes, parsley can also be deep fried. Wash the parsley and remove the stalks, then dry thoroughly to avoid the fat spitting. Cook quickly in medium-hot fat – not too hot or the fresh green colour will be lost – and only a little at a time otherwise it might go soggy. Drain on kitchen paper and serve immediately.

PARSLEY SAUCE

This is probably the best known way of using parsley in the kitchen and the creamy sauce with its subtle tang makes a particularly good accompaniment to white fish.

50 g (2 oz) butter
40 g (1$\frac{1}{2}$ oz) flour
900 ml (1$\frac{1}{2}$ pt) chicken stock or milk
600 ml (4 tbsp) chopped fresh parsley
Juice of 1 lemon (about 45 ml/3 tbsp)
Sea salt and freshly ground black pepper

Melt the butter in a small saucepan and stir in the flour to make a crumbly paste. Cook for 1 minute then remove pan from heat and gradually add the stock or milk. (If there are any juices available from the accompanying fish dish, these can also be added.) Return the pan to the heat and bring to the boil, stirring continuously, until the sauce is thick and smooth. Remove from the heat and add the finely chopped parsley. Slowly stir in the lemon juice and season with salt and pepper to taste.

PARSLEY BUTTER

This adds a pretty finishing touch to grilled fish or meat and tastes delicious.

125 g ($\frac{1}{4}$ lb) butter
1 clove garlic
45 ml (3 tbsp) chopped fresh parsley
15 ml (1 tbsp) lemon juice
Sea salt and freshly ground black pepper

Cream the butter in a bowl until smooth. Peel and crush the garlic and blend well into the butter. Add the finely chopped parsley and mix in thoroughly. Season with the lemon juice and salt and pepper. Form into little pats and chill until firm.

POTATO AND PARSLEY CAKES
(makes about 14 cakes)
This is a tasty way of using up left-over potatoes. Adjust the quantities to suit the amount of potatoes you have.

2 eggs
60 ml (4 tbsp) chopped fresh parsley
125 g (4 oz) grated cheese
700 g (1$\frac{1}{2}$ lb) mashed potatoes
Sea salt and freshly ground black pepper
125 g (4 oz) fresh breadcrumbs
25 g (1 oz) butter
90 ml (6 tbsp) olive oil

Beat the eggs and add them with the parsley and cheese to the mashed potatoes. Mix well and season with salt and pepper. Form into flat cakes with a spoon and coat with breadcrumbs. Heat some of the butter and oil in a heavy frying pan until the butter is beginning to sizzle. Add as many cakes as will fit the pan without crowding and fry until the underside is crisp, then turn them over and fry the other side. Remove and keep warm. Repeat the process with the rest of the oil, butter and remaining cakes.

Armoracia rusticana

HORSERADISH

Family: Cruciferae

'With a little vinegar is commonly used among the Germans
for sauce to eat fish with, and such like meats, as we do
mustard but this kind of sauce doth heat the stomach better
and causeth better digestion than mustard.'
– John Gerard

A member of the mustard family, horseradish is probably the most sharp tasting of all our herbs. It is one of the herbs used by the Jewish people at the time of the Passover and although now best known for its use as a sauce to accompany beef, it has many medicinal as well as nutritional properties. During the Middle Ages it was known as 'scurvy grass' and was used not only as a digestive aid but also crushed and applied externally to ease aching limbs and joints.

Horseradish is a native of the muddy swamplands of southern Europe and western Asia and was introduced to the rest of Europe in the thirteenth century. It now grows wild as a weed in much of Europe and North America. A hardy perennial, at maturity it will reach a height of 60–90 cm (2–3 ft) and has large dark green floppy leaves and a single stem which bears white flowers. The leaves vary in shape from deeply toothed to smooth-edged and the flowers may not appear every year.

Cultivation

Because of its long, searching taproot, horseradish will only thrive on a deeply dug soil and preferably one that is cool, moist and free from stones, so prepare the ground by digging to about 60 cm (2 ft) and lightening the soil with humus if it is full of clay. Propagate by cuttings taken from the root and plant them about 2.5 cm (1 in) deep in a sunny position. Keep well watered until the seedling is fully developed. Horseradish can easily get out of control so restrict it to the less formal part of the garden and prevent its invasive growth by either sinking tiles around the long taproot or placing the cuttings by a wall or in an old ceramic pipe or drain. Remember also to keep a watch for snails which have a particular liking for

horseradish and will strip a plant bare within a few days. When the flowers appear, remove them in order to conserve the goodness of the plant in the root. This is the part which is useful, and can be dried

Horseradish

Dittander and Pepperwort

Annual Dittander

and stored. For this purpose, the white taproot should be dug up at the end of the first season, cleaned and shredded into 5 cm (2 in) lengths which can then be put in a very cool oven 110°C/225°F (gas $\frac{1}{4}$) to dry. When they are completely brittle, take them out, allow to cool and then store in a screw-topped jar ready to be crushed when needed.

Uses

Medicinally, a poultice of freshly grated horseradish root applied to insect bites and stings will ease the pain and reduce inflammation. Mixed into a paste with water and massaged on to stiff or aching joints and limbs, it will bring rapid relief, and the same mixture can be applied to help heal chilblains – provided that they are not broken. Like garlic, horse-radish is supposed to rid an animal of worms but it is usually very difficult to persuade the animal to eat food containing it!

Because of its high vitamin C content, horseradish is valuable in the kitchen, and a small amount added to the diet regularly will also help purify the blood and cleanse the body of excess mucus – particularly beneficial for anyone suffering from nasal congestion or sinusitis. Use a little grated root to add flavouring to coleslaw and vegetable salads or add it to cream cheese as a tasty sandwich filling.

HORSERADISH SAUCE

This famous accompaniment to beef is also delicious mixed with cooked cranberries and served with game.

60 ml (4 tbsp) grated horseradish
10 ml (2 tsp) dry mustard
5 ml (1 tsp) wine vinegar
60 ml (4 tbsp) double cream (or natural yoghurt)

Mix the horseradish, mustard and vinegar together. Add the cream and blend until smooth. Serve cold.

Armoracia rusticana

Anethum graveolens

DILL

Family: Umbelliferae

'That being burnt and laid upon moist ulcers
it cureth them.'
– John Gerard

The English name 'dill' comes from the Saxon word 'dilla', to lull, and this herb has been used from the time of ancient Egyptian civilization as a powerful digestive tranquillizer. It originated in the Mediterranean countries and parts of Scandinavia, and has always been associated with witchcraft and the occult. In England it was one of the herbs traditionally gathered on St John's Eve to be taken home as a protection from witches and evil spirits. Apart from its medicinal and magic powers, dill has a distinctive flavour, similar to fennel, which makes it useful in the kitchen.

Like all members of the Umbelliferae family, dill makes an attractive addition to the herb garden. It will grow to about 60 cm (2 ft) in height and has finely divided leaves that are as feathery as those of fennel but lighter in colour, and again like fennel it bears umbels of yellow flowers, which appear in late spring to early summer.

Cultivation

Dill will tolerate almost any soil as long as it is well-drained, but it does prefer sunshine and should never be allowed to dry out. Grow from seeds, which should be sown in a well-raked bed in the early spring, pressed gently and not too deeply into the soil. Continue planting seeds throughout the summer if you want to ensure a continuous supply of dill leaves. The seedlings should be separated out as soon as they are large enough to handle, leaving about 25 cm (10 in) between plants and keeping them well watered Avoid planting near fennel, coriander or angelica because they will cross-pollinate and their flavours will be lost. The plant will grow quickly and will

produce a large supply of leaves before the flowers appear. Harvest these when the plant is about 25 cm (10 in) high and snip a few leaves off regularly until the late autumn. All the strength of the plant will go into forming the seeds, so if you are growing dill primarily for its leaves make sure they are picked before the plant flowers. The seeds, which are flat and brownish when ripe, should be gathered when both flowers and seeds are on the plant if they are to be used for pickling; if they are to be kept for propagation – and dill seeds are very prolific – leave them on the plant until they turn brown.

Dill can be grown indoors but being a large plant it will need plenty of room and it will not grow to form seeds. An outdoor plant will, however, provide seeds that retain their germinating power for up to 10 years and should provide more than enough seeds for a continuous supply for indoor growing. Under ideal conditions dill's unusually delicate tap root will grow to a depth of 60 cm (2 ft) but fortunately it will not grow so enthusiastically indoors! Use a 15 cm (6 in) pot filled with light compost, distribute about six seeds on to the surface of the soil, and then press them down lightly. Cover the pot with a plastic bag and put in a dark place at a temperature of about 20°C/70°F. The seeds should germinate in about 10 days and once the seedlings have appeared, place the pot in a sunny position or at least somewhere that is well-lit and avoid letting the soil become dry. Once the seedlings are established, they should be placed in individual pots. Fertilize the young plants with a nitrogen-rich fertilizer because they take a lot of nutrients from the soil and always leave about 10 cm (4 in) of stem when you trim the tips for use in the kitchen.

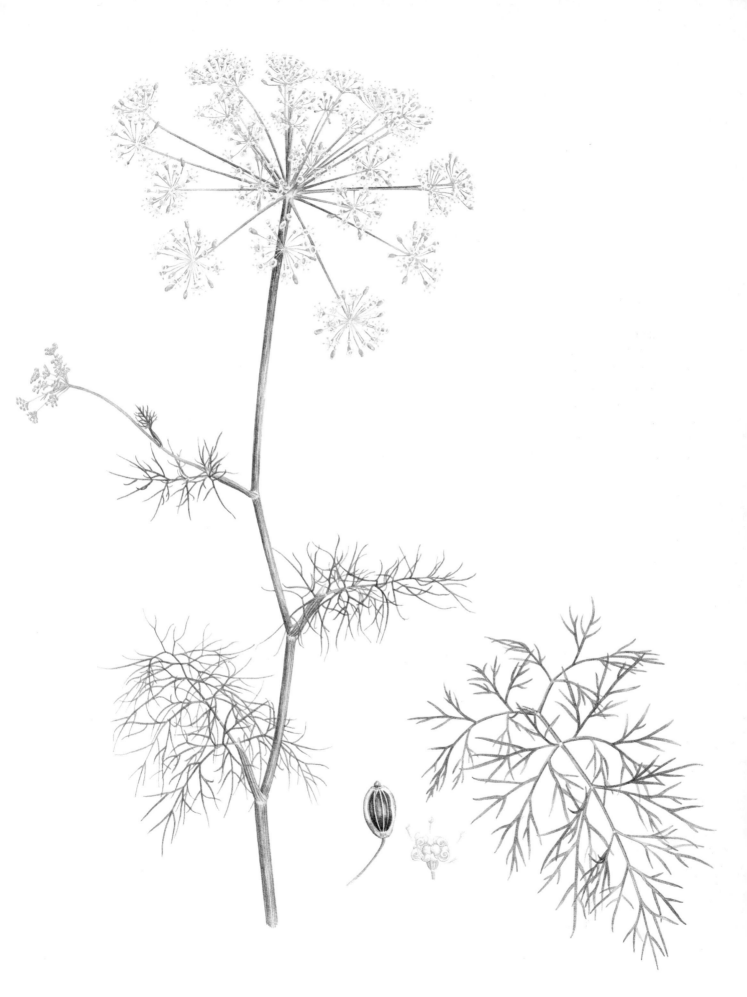

Anethum graveolens

Uses

Dill is as useful medicinally today as it was in the past. It is particularly good for strengthening the nails because it is full of silicic acid which asists nail growth. Chew a few dill seeds regularly if you have problems with brittle nails – it will also ensure sweet breath – and drink a cup of dill tea each evening. This can be made by infusing 5 ml (1 tsp) of crushed dill seeds in a cup of boiling water. The remedy will be even more effective if you also add 5 ml (1 tsp) of gelatine or a jelly cube to the tea instead of sugar.

Both the leaves (called dill weed) and seeds are used in the kitchen, but the leaves do not dry well and the only way to preserve them is to freeze them in small batches that are individually wrapped. The plant has a mild aniseed flavour reminiscent of fennel but less obvious, and small snippings of the fresh leaves make a delicious garnish for savoury dishes such as scrambled eggs or cottage cheese. They are also good sprinkled on white soups just before serving and the flavour goes particularly well with fish. Try sprinkling dill leaves over salmon before grilling or use them to make a basting sauce for mackerel or fried fish. Scandinavians frequently use dill to decorate their smörgåsbord, and the herb is popular with cooks everywhere as a pickling ingredient.

DILL BISCUITS

Whole or ground dill seeds make a subtle difference to home-made bread and biscuits, adding a flavour that is milder than caraway.

450 ml ($\frac{3}{4}$ pt) milk
50 g (2 oz) butter
550 g (1 lb 4 oz) plain flour
15 ml (1 tbsp) brown sugar
45 ml (3 tbsp) dill seeds
25 g (1 oz) fresh or 20 ml (4 tsp) dried yeast
15 ml (1 tbsp) salt
2 eggs, beaten

Bring milk to the boil and add butter. Allow to cool. Sift dry ingredients. Dissolve the yeast in a little warm water. Add the egg and the cooled milk. Gradually mix in the dry ingredients and knead well until a dough is formed. Cover with a clean cloth and allow to rise for 30 minutes. Grease two baking trays. When dough has doubled in size roll out on a lightly floured surface and cut into biscuit shapes. Allow to prove in a warm place for 30 minutes, brush with little milk, sprinkle with extra dill seeds and bake at the top of the oven preheated for 200°C/400°F (gas 6) for 15 minutes.

PICKLED CUCUMBERS WITH DILL

Dill leaves
Pickle: 4.5 kg (10 lb) small cucumbers
       2 peppercorns
       4 cloves
       4 allspice
       5 ml (1 tsp) mustard seed
4.5 litres (1 gallon) water
200 ml ($\frac{1}{3}$ pt) sea salt
200 ml ($\frac{1}{3}$ pt) malt vinegar

Place a layer of dill leaves in a sealable jar or crock. Add small cucumbers, dill leaves and pickle in layers until the jar is almost full. Add the salt and malt vinegar to the water and pour into the jar until it is filled completely. Cover the jar and allow to stand for 2 weeks. Remove the cucumbers and pack into sterile pickling jars or pots. Bring the brine to the boil and add a little more dill. Fill the pickling jars to the brim with the brine and seal.

DILL WATER

Sipped twice a day, preferably after meals, dill water will help assimilate food and generally aid digestion. It will also calm hiccups and induce restful sleep, and is particularly good for children as it does not contain harmful drugs.

25 g (1 oz) ripe dill seeds
300 ml ($\frac{1}{2}$ pt) hot water
15 ml (1 tbsp) clear honey

Crush the seeds well with a pestle and mortar and soak for 3 or 4 hours in the water. Strain and sweeten with honey.

Sambucus nigra

ELDER

Family: Caprifoliaceae

'If the medical properties of its leaves, bark and berries were
fully known, I cannot tell what our countryman could ail for
which he might not fetch a remedy from every hedge,
either for sickness or wounds.'
– John Evelyn

There are countless legends associated with this useful herb, which grows wild along the hedgerows of Europe, North America and Asia. It has long been linked with the occult, and in Nordic countries it is believed to be guarded by the dryad, Hylde-Moer, who must first be invoked before any part of the tree is cut down. Failure to do so results in a lifetime of haunting by the spirit. Tradition also has it that he who stands beneath the elder tree on midsummer eve will see the king of fairyland and all his courtiers pass by. The botanical name for elder – *Sambucus* – is the Greek for stringed instrument and in fact pipes and whistles are still made from the hollow stems today.

Elder is a hardy deciduous shrub. The European variety will grow to 7 m (23 ft); the smaller American variety reaches 3 m (12 ft). The strongly scented clusters (heads) of tiny white blossom appear from May and last for about 2 months to be followed by the deep purple elderberries which ripen at the end of the summer.

Cultivation

Elder bushes are easy to grow and will thrive on any reasonable soil although they prefer a sunny, moist position. The quickest way to propagate is by taking cuttings from leafless shoots in the early autumn for planting out the following spring. (Growing from seed is difficult and hardly worth the time as the seeds are very slow to grow.) In the late autumn or early spring the bushes should be pruned back to keep their shape and to encourage young growth.

Uses

There are many uses for elder, medicinal, cosmetic and culinary. The berries contain a high quantity of vitamin C and can be used to make a soothing cough and cold syrup. A tisane made from the flowers will induce sleep, and when applied externally will have a soothing effect on burns and scalds.

To help clear up acne and spots, apply a poultice of crushed elderflowers: tie about 5 ml (1 tsp) of fresh elderflowers firmly in a muslin bag and hold in a little

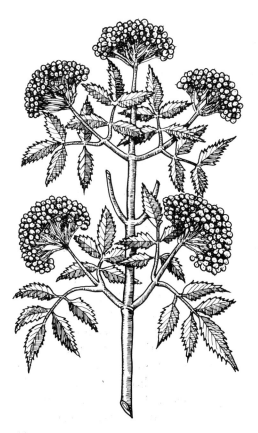

Common Elder tree

Elder with white berries

Harts Elder or Cluster Elder

boiling water until softened. Apply to the affected area as hot as is bearable; soak again and reapply several times until the goodness of the herb is used up. To prevent spots from recurring, use an elderflower cleanser, which will have the added benefit of softening the skin and fading unwanted freckles. To make the cleanser, add a cup of boiling water to 5 ml (1 tsp) of dried flowers or 15 ml (1 tbsp) of fresh and allow to steep for at least 30 minutes.

ELDERFLOWER CORDIAL

This cordial is particularly refreshing on a hot summer day when served with ice.

Thinly peeled rind of 1 lemon
50 g (2 oz) brown sugar
3 fresh elderflower heads
300 ml ($\frac{1}{2}$ pt) boiling water

Put the lemon rind, sugar and elderflowers in a large jug and pour the boiling water over. Stir until the sugar has completely dissolved and allow to cool. Strain, then dilute to taste with cold water and ice.

ELDERFLOWER JELLY

1.75 kg (4 lb) cooking apples
1.2 litres (2 pt) water
1 kg (2.2 lb) preserving sugar
4 large elderflower heads
45 ml (3 tbsp) lemon juice

Wash and chop the apples and without peeling or coring them. Place in a preserving pan filled with the water. Bring to the boil and simmer until the apples are soft. Pour into a muslin bag, or jelly bag if available, and allow the juice to drip through slowly – overnight if necessary. Measure the extracted juice and to each 600 ml (1 pt) add 450 g (1 lb) of sugar. Bring the liquid to the boil. Wash the elderflowers and tie them in a muslin bag. Add to the liquid and continue to boil for 10 minutes. Remove the flowers and boil for a further 10 minutes until setting point is reached. (To test this, remove the pan from the boil and take a little jelly and put it on a cool plate; if a skin forms after 5 minutes and the liquid begins to solidify, setting point has been reached.) Skim the liquid and add the lemon juice. Pour into hot sterilised jars and seal.

Sambucas niger

GARLIC

Family: Liliaceae

'It performs almost miracles in phlegmatic habits of the body.'
– Culpeper

Garlic is one of the oldest and most valued of our cultivated plants. Its fame as a medicinal and culinary herb with almost magical powers was passed from the Egyptians to the Greeks and from them to the Romans, who were responsible for bringing garlic to Britain. It is said to have been eaten by the labourers who built the pyramids of Egypt and by Roman soldiers on long marches in order to keep up their strength, and it is mentioned in both the Old and New Testaments of the Bible as being one of the herbs used to embalm the dead. Together with hyssop, garlic was considered a cure for leprosy and in the Middle Ages lepers were commonly known as 'pilgarlics' because they were often to be seen peeling garlic cloves. The herb has also long been considered to have the power to ward off evil and is used today by the Chinese, Arabs and Egyptians to exorcise evil spirits. Cloves of garlic are sliced and hung up in each room of the house at night, then taken down, burned and replaced by fresh ones in the morning, until the home is felt to be free of evil. Garlic is no less legendary in Europe where, as everyone knows, it will protect the sleeper from vampire bites in the dead of night.

Garlic is a member of the onion family and very strongly scented, particularly in the bulb, which consists of several bulblets or cloves enclosed in a white membrane. The plant is a perennial which will probably reach about 60 cm (2 ft) in height. The thin, tubular leaves are similar to those of the spring onion, and the upright stem will bear tiny whitish flowers in a large cluster during spring and summer.

Cultivation

Although garlic favours a warm Mediterranean climate, it will survive quite happily in a colder climate like Britain's given a little care. Choose a warm, sunny spot and prepare the soil as you would for an onion bed by digging in plenty of manure and compost, and forking over several times to make sure that the soil is fine. Plant the cloves in the spring (buy them from a seed merchant or from the green-grocer, whichever is the cheaper) and try to leave about 15 cm (6 in) between each plant to give them room to spread. Do not cover them with too much soil – about 2 cm ($\frac{3}{4}$ in) should be sufficient – and water them every few days, checking that they have not uprooted themselves. Collect the garlic bulbs in the autumn when the tops of the plant have died back thoroughly. Lift the plant carefully and let it dry indoors or somewhere under cover, ready for use in the winter and following spring. The plants look very effective in the kitchen if they are plaited together and strung on the wall.

Garlic can also be grown quite successfully indoors but it will not develop as many offshoots and the cloves will not last for more than a few months. It is worth growing indoors anyway for an easily accessible supply of the tasty green leaves. Use well-developed cloves and plant them individually in pots, covering each clove to about half way up with compost and watering moderately. They will soon start to shoot and they may even flower.

Uses

Garlic is an antiseptic whose powers range from curing diarrhoea, gout and hot flushes to relieving tension. It can be rubbed on to unbroken chilblains to ease the irritation, and a drink made from a well-crushed garlic clove simmered in 300 ml ($\frac{1}{2}$ pt) of milk for about 10 minutes can be sipped to relieve a dry hacking cough. A little garlic in the daily diet of children and domestic animals is said to prevent them catching worms, though you may have difficulty convincing pets of the benefits of garlic-flavoured food. In any case garlic is a *must* in the kitchen. Apart from being a valuable aid to digestion, it is an essential ingredient in many recipes, both simple and complicated, and even the merest suggestion of this delicious herb will improve many a bland dish. If you find the taste very strong, cut a clove in half and use the exposed surface to rub round your cooking vessel or salad bowl to give a distinctive but more delicate taste.

GARLIC BREAD
Split a French loaf lengthways and butter both cut edges generously. Crush 3 or 4 garlic cloves and spread them over the butter. Garnish with chopped parsley, wedge the two slices together and wrap the loaf in foil, securing all the edges. Bake in a very slow oven 140°C/275°F (gas 1), for 15–30 minutes until the butter has melted and oozed well into the hot bread.

FRENCH ONION SOUP (serves 4)
Garlic is particularly beloved by the French and is an essential ingredient in their delicious onion soup.

900 g (2 lb) onions, peeled and sliced
2 cloves of garlic, crushed
50 g (2 oz) butter
15 ml (1 tbsp) olive oil
7.5 ml (1½ tsp) flour
1.1 litre (2 pt) stock (chicken or beef)
Salt and pepper
50 g (2 oz) cheese, finely grated

Sauté the onions and garlic in a heavy-based pan for three minutes. Add oil and flour and cook gently for a further minute. Gradually add stock, and season. Simmer gently for 30 minutes until the onions are tender. Serve sprinkled with finely grated cheese, and accompanied by French bread, either fresh, or buttered and baked in a moderate oven, or by Garlic Bread as in the recipe above.

BEEF CASSEROLE WITH GARLIC (serves 4)

30 ml (2 tbsp) oil
2 cloves garlic, peeled
700 g (1½ lb) lean stewing steak, cut into pieces
1 small green pepper, sliced
300 ml (½ pt) tomato juice
1 sprig dried thyme
5 ml (1 tsp) salt

Heat the oil in a casserole and gently sauté the garlic in it. Add the meat and brown on all sides. Add the green pepper, fry for a few minutes and then add the tomato juice to cover the meat. Finally add the thyme and season with salt. Cover and simmer for 2 hours at 150°C/300°F (gas 2) until the meat is tender. Remove the sprig of thyme before serving. Jacket or mashed potatoes or boiled rice go well with this.

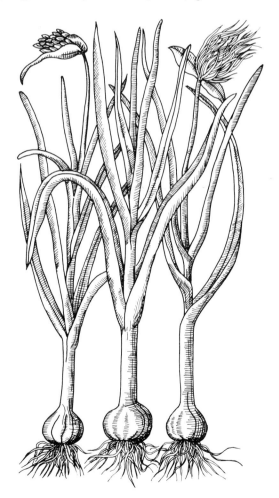

Garlic

Helichrysum augustifolium

CURRY PLANT

Family: Compositae

A remedy against the stuffing of the head, that
commeth through coldness of the brain, if a garland
thereof be put about the head.'
– John Gerard

A native of central and southern Italy, this attractive and delicately perfumed shrub is an asset to any herb garden. Curry plant is one of the least familiar perennial herbs in Britain although it is very easy to grow, thriving on dry, stony soils and forming a dense, conical-shaped grey bush which, upon maturity, will reach 40 cm/15 in in height. The plant produces a multitude of tiny branches which spring from its centre bearing soft, grey, downy leaves that are thin and spikey. The small, yellow flowers appear in late spring and last until the beginning of autumn. When dried. they retain their colour and faintly spicey aroma.

The whole curry plant contains caffeic acid and a complex essential oil that is used as a diuretic and is most beneficial in the treatment of diseases of the respiratory passages, gall bladder and liver. An infusion of the leaves of curry plant will ease rheumatism and soothe many allergic conditions.

Although not often used in cooking, a sprig of curry plant is delicious when incorporated into some chicken or egg dishes.

CHICKEN KIEV WITH CURRY PLANT
(serves 4)

4 boneless chicken breasts
125 g (4 oz) softened butter
30 ml (2 tbsp) fresh parsley, chopped
10 ml (2 tsp) chopped curry plant
2 large cloves garlic, crushed
3 eggs, beaten
175 g (6 oz) fresh fine white breadcrumbs
oil for deep frying

Place the chicken breasts between sheets of greaseproof paper and flatten with a rolling pin, form into rolls and chill in refrigerator. Blend the butter, parsley, curry plant and garlic and fill each chicken breast with the mixture and secure firmly with a skewer if necessary. Dip into beaten egg mixture and coat with breadcrumbs. Repeat several times for each portion. Chill thoroughly, remove any skewers and deep fry one or two at a time for 7–8 minutes until cooked and golden brown, keeping cooked portions hot. Remember that when the chicken flesh is pierced the hot butter can come spurting out!

Helichrysum angustifolium

Achillea millefolium

YARROW

Family : Compositae

'Venus governs this useful plant'
– Culpeper

Yarrow is one of the most ancient of our herbs and according to legend was dedicated to the devil. It is still used nowadays by the Chinese when consulting the "I Ching" or "Book of Changes" and in Europe the superstitious will place it under their pillows for dreams of a future spouse. Yarrow has long been valued for its antiseptic properties – it was frequently carried by soldiers who would apply it to their battle wounds to speed recovery.

Cultivation

Yarrow is a very hardy perennial which grows wild all over Europe. A mature plant will form an attractive bushy clump reaching 60 cm/2 ft in height with dark green feather leaves and clusters of tiny pinkish-white florets that bloom throughout the summer on ribbed, upright stems. The whole plant emits a refreshingly strong perfume when crushed and is usually surrounded by bees.

A common wayside plant, yarrow will readily grow on any soil and in any position – take care when transplanting to your herb garden to restrict the roots or it will quickly spread and swamp the less robust herbs. Once established it will enhance the flavour and perfume of neighbouring herbs and help them to resist disease.

Uses

Yarrow, or to use its common and more appropriate name, Sneezewort, was used long ago as snuff because its application promoted sneezing and was therefore valued as an antidote for headaches. A tea, made with 25g (1 oz) dried yarrow flowers and 600 ml (1 pt) boiling water, if taken while still warm will ease a head-cold, act as a tonic and stimulant and

is sometimes even used to relieve the pain of angina. A diuretic, it can be used to help slimmers, reduce fever and is also good for cramp.

The whole of the yarrow plant, except the roots, is beneficial to man, not only medicinally, but also cosmetically. Used as a cleanser and astringent it is invaluable, particularly for those with greasy skins and thread veins. Allow 5 ml (1 tsp) of the dried, crushed herb to infuse for about 30 minutes in 150 ml ($\frac{1}{4}$ pt) boiling water and apply it while still fresh. Add the remainder to the bath to help you relax.

Culinary

Although yarrow leaves are pleasantly flavoured, they can be strong. Experiment by adding them fresh to salads and cheese sandwiches for extra flavour.

Red Flowered Yarrow

Achillea millefolium

INDEX

The publishers would like to thank Justin de Blank for their tireless search for the herbs that flowered early and thus enabled the artist to keep drawing during the long winter months. A special thank you is also due to Zane Carey whose late help enabled the book to be published on time.